ECUMENICAL
CREEDS
AND
REFORMED
CONFESSIONS

D0469562

FAITH
ALIVE®
Christian Resources

Grand Rapids, Michigan

Ecumenical creeds and reformed confessions.
   1. Reformed Church—creeds. 2. Christian Reformed Church—
Creeds. 3. Creeds, Ecumenical. I. Christian Reformed Church.
BX9428.A1E28   1987   238'.6731   87-18222
ISBN 978-0-930265-34-2

15 14 13 12 11 10

CONTENTS

PREFACE 5

ECUMENICAL CREEDS
   Apostles' Creed 7
   Nicene Creed 8
   Athanasian Creed 9

REFORMED CONFESSIONS
   Heidelberg Catechism 12
   Belgic Confession 78
   Canons of Dort 122

HARMONY OF THE CONFESSIONS 146

PREFACE

The three short documents in the first part of this booklet are *ecumenical* creeds: Apostles' Creed, Nicene Creed, and Athanasian Creed. Each of them, written long before the church divided into various branches, is accepted by most Christian churches. (Catholic and Protestant churches use all three creeds; the Orthodox church accepts only the Nicene.)

The three longer documents in the latter part are distinctively *Reformed* confessions: Heidelberg Catechism, Belgic Confession, and Canons of Dort. Typically Protestant statements of faith, they were written at the time when divisions among Protestants were becoming permanent. Thus, they belong to that family of Reformed and Presbyterian creeds which also includes the Westminster, Gallican, and Scottish Confessions.

Statements of faith by God's people have tended to become longer as time passes. The typical Old Testament statement is only two Bible verses in length (Deut. 6:4–5). Those imbedded in the New Testament run from a few lines (1 Tim. 3:16) to several verses (Col. 1:15–20). The creeds of the ancient church, such as the Apostles' Creed, are longer yet; and the Reformation creeds have almost become short books. (The Westminster Confession, for example, is much longer than any of the three confessions included here.)

Creeds have usually emerged during major turning points in the history of the church, particularly during four critical periods when it was necessary for the church to differentiate itself from others in its environment. The first such turning point was Israel's division from the nations in her exodus from Egypt. Moses defined Israel's monotheistic faith in the *shema* of Deuteronomy 6 ("Hear, O Israel: The LORD our God is one LORD").

The second turning point came with Christ. Writers of the New Testament wanted to distinguish the infant church's understanding of Christ from the views of its Jewish mother, and they often incorporated short summaries of that faith in their writings.

Documents in this booklet represent statements of faith from the third and fourth critical turning points. The ecumenical creeds represent the ways in which the ancient church defined its faith in a Gentile world rich in competing philosophies and religions. And the Reformed confessions show how this branch of Protestantism differentiated itself not only from Roman Catholicism, but also from the other families of Protestant churches.

The *Apostles' Creed* was not written by the apostles; it is the culmination of several centuries of reflection on the meaning of the

Christian faith. The ancient church used this creed to identify believers, to instruct new converts, and to provide a unifying confession of faith for worship and liturgy. The *Nicene Creed* is the church's response, partly based on the Apostles' Creed, to a particularly dangerous set of teachings (Arianism) which would have masked the identity of Christ. And, because its unique phrases are meant more to defend than explain the faith, the Nicene Creed has always been used more for teaching than for worship. The *Athanasian Creed* (quite certainly Athanasius did not write it) is the latest of the ecumenical creeds, dating back to the early Dark Ages. Though seldom used in worship, it is one of the clearest definitions of the Trinity and the incarnation ever written.

The *Heidelberg Catechism* (1563) originated in one of the few pockets of Calvinistic faith in the Lutheran and Catholic territories of Germany. Conceived originally as a teaching instrument to promote religious unity in the Palatinate, the catechism soon became a guide for preaching as well. It is a remarkably warm-hearted and personalized confession of faith, eminently deserving of its popularity among Reformed churches to the present day.

The *Belgic Confession* (1561) owes its origin to the need for a clear and comprehensive statement of Reformed faith during the time of the Spanish inquisition in the Lowlands. Guido de Brès, its primary author, was pleading for understanding and toleration from King Philip II of Spain who was determined to root out all Protestant factions in his jurisdiction. Hence, this confession takes pains to point out the continuity of Reformed belief with that of the ancient Christian creeds, as well as to differentiate it from Catholic belief (on the one hand), and from Anabaptist teachings (on the other).

The *Canons of Dort* come from an international synod of Reformed people held in Dordrecht, Netherlands, in 1618–19. While the synod accomplished many other things as well, one of its main purposes was to adjudicate a theological controversy (Arminianism) concerning the way in which believers receive the benefit of Christ. The canons, therefore, are polemic in purpose, articulating Calvinistic beliefs in direct rebuttal of Arminianism. This confession is a very finely tuned piece of theological writing, ably delineating a biblically Reformed perspective on matters central to Christian life and experience.

Apostles' Creed

I believe in God, the Father almighty,
   creator of heaven and earth.

I believe in Jesus Christ, his only Son, our Lord,
   who was conceived by the Holy Spirit
   and born of the virgin Mary.
   He suffered under Pontius Pilate,
   was crucified, died, and was buried;
   he descended to hell.
   The third day he rose again from the dead.
   He ascended to heaven
   and is seated at the right hand of God the Father almighty.
   From there he will come to judge the living and the dead.

I believe in the Holy Spirit,
   the holy catholic* church,
   the communion of saints,
   the forgiveness of sins,
   the resurrection of the body,
   and the life everlasting. Amen.

*that is, the true Christian church of all times and all places

This creed is called the *Apostles' Creed* not because it was produced by the apostles themselves but because it contains a brief summary of their teachings. It sets forth their doctrine "in sublime simplicity, in unsurpassable brevity, in beautiful order, and with liturgical solemnity." In its present form it is dated no later than the fourth century. More than any other Christian creed, it may justly be called an ecumenical symbol of faith. This translation of the Latin text was approved by the CRC Synod of 1988.

Nicene Creed

We believe in one God,
> the Father almighty,
> maker of heaven and earth,
> of all things visible and invisible.

And in one Lord Jesus Christ,
> the only Son of God,
> begotten from the Father before all ages,
> > God from God,
> > Light from Light,
> > true God from true God,
> begotten, not made;
> of the same essence as the Father.
> Through him all things were made.
> For us and for our salvation
> > he came down from heaven;
> > he became incarnate by the Holy Spirit and the virgin Mary,
> > and was made human.
> > He was crucified for us under Pontius Pilate;
> > he suffered and was buried.
> > The third day he rose again, according to the Scriptures.
> > He ascended to heaven
> > and is seated at the right hand of the Father.
> > He will come again with glory
> > to judge the living and the dead.
> > His kingdom will never end.

And we believe in the Holy Spirit,
> the Lord, the giver of life.
> He proceeds from the Father and the Son,
> and with the Father and the Son is worshiped and glorified.
> He spoke through the prophets.
> We believe in one holy catholic and apostolic church.
> We affirm one baptism for the forgiveness of sins.
> We look forward to the resurrection of the dead,
> and to life in the world to come. Amen.

The Nicene Creed, also called the Nicaeno-Constantinopolitan Creed, is a statement of the orthodox faith of the early Christian church in opposition to certain heresies, especially Arianism. These heresies, which disturbed the church during the fourth century, concerned the doctrine of the trinity and of the person of Christ. Both the Greek (Eastern) and the Latin (Western) church held this creed in honor, though with one important difference: the Western church insisted on the inclusion of the phrase *and the Son* (known as the *filioque*) in the article on the procession of the Holy Spirit; this phrase still is repudiated by the Eastern Orthodox church. In its present form this creed goes back partially to the Council of Nicea (A.D. 325) with additions by the Council of Constantinople (A.D. 381). It was accepted in its present form at the Council of Chalcedon in 451, but the *filioque* phrase was not added until 589. However, the creed is in substance an accurate and majestic formulation of the Nicene faith. This translation of the Greek text was approved by the CRC Synod of 1988.

Athanasian Creed

Whoever desires to be saved should above all
hold to the catholic faith.
Anyone who does not keep it whole and unbroken
will doubtless perish eternally.

Now this is the catholic faith:

That we worship one God in trinity
and the trinity in unity,
neither blending their persons
nor dividing their essence.
For the person of the Father is a distinct person,
the person of the Son is another,
and that of the Holy Spirit still another.
But the divinity of the Father, Son, and Holy Spirit is one,
their glory equal, their majesty coeternal.

What quality the Father has, the Son has, and the Holy Spirit has.
The Father is uncreated,
the Son is uncreated,
the Holy Spirit is uncreated.

The Father is immeasurable,
the Son is immeasurable,
the Holy Spirit is immeasurable.

The Father is eternal,
the Son is eternal,
the Holy Spirit is eternal.

And yet there are not three eternal beings;
there is but one eternal being.
So too there are not three uncreated or immeasurable beings;
there is but one uncreated and immeasurable being.

Similarly, the Father is almighty,
the Son is almighty,
the Holy Spirit is almighty.
Yet there are not three almighty beings;
there is but one almighty being.

Thus the Father is God,
the Son is God,
the Holy Spirit is God.
Yet there are not three gods;
there is but one God.

Thus the Father is Lord,
the Son is Lord,
the Holy Spirit is Lord.
Yet there are not three lords;
there is but one Lord.

Just as Christian truth compels us
to confess each person individually
as both God and Lord,
so catholic religion forbids us
to say that there are three gods or lords.

This creed is named after Athanasius (A.D. 293–373), the champion of orthodoxy against Arian attacks on the doctrine of the trinity. Although Athanasius did not write this creed and it is improperly named after him, the name persists because until the seventeenth century it was commonly ascribed to him. It is not from Greek (Eastern), but from Latin (Western) origin, and is not recognized by the Eastern Orthodox Church today. Apart from the opening and closing sentences, this creed consists of two parts, the first setting forth the orthodox doctrine of the trinity, and the second dealing chiefly with the incarnation and the two-natures doctrine. The translation above was adopted by the CRC Synod of 1988.

The Father was neither made nor created nor begotten from anyone.
The Son was neither made nor created;
he was begotten from the Father alone.
The Holy Spirit was neither made nor created nor begotten;
he proceeds from the Father and the Son.

Accordingly there is one Father, not three fathers;
there is one Son, not three sons;
there is one Holy Spirit, not three holy spirits.

Nothing in this trinity is before or after,
nothing is greater or smaller;
in their entirety the three persons
are coeternal and coequal with each other.

So in everything, as was said earlier,
we must worship their trinity in their unity
and their unity in their trinity.

Anyone then who desires to be saved
should think thus about the trinity.

But it is necessary for eternal salvation
that one also believe in the incarnation
of our Lord Jesus Christ faithfully.

Now this is the true faith:

That we believe and confess
that our Lord Jesus Christ, God's Son,
is both God and human, equally.

He is God from the essence of the Father,
begotten before time;
and he is human from the essence of his mother,
born in time;
completely God, completely human,
with a rational soul and human flesh;
equal to the Father as regards divinity,
less than the Father as regards humanity.

Although he is God and human,
yet Christ is not two, but one.
He is one, however,
not by his divinity being turned into flesh,
but by God's taking humanity to himself.

He is one,
certainly not by the blending of his essence,
but by the unity of his person.
For just as one human is both rational soul and flesh,
so too the one Christ is both God and human.

He suffered for our salvation;
he descended to hell;
he arose from the dead;
he ascended to heaven;
he is seated at the Father's right hand;
from there he will come to judge the living and the dead.
At his coming all people will arise bodily
and give an accounting of their own deeds.
Those who have done good will enter eternal life,
and those who have done evil will enter eternal fire.

This is the catholic faith:
one cannot be saved without believing it firmly and faithfully.

The Heidelberg Catechism

The Heidelberg Catechism was composed in Heidelberg at the request of Elector Frederick III, who ruled the Palatinate, an influential German province, from 1559 to 1576. An old tradition credits Zacharius Ursinus and Caspar Olevianus with being coauthors of the new catechism. Both were certainly involved in its composition, although one of them may have had primary responsibility. All we know for sure is reported by the Elector in his preface of January 19, 1563. It was, he writes, "with the advice and cooperation of our entire theological faculty in this place, and of all superintendents and distinguished servants of the church" that he secured the preparation of the Heidelberg Catechism. The catechism was approved by a synod in Heidelberg in January 1563. A second and third German edition, each with small additions, as well as a Latin translation were published the same year in Heidelberg. Soon the catechism was divided into fifty-two sections so that one Lord's Day could be explained in preaching each Sunday of the year.

The Synod of Dort in 1618–1619 approved the Heidelberg Catechism, and it soon became the most ecumenical of the Reformed catechisms and confessions. The catechism has been translated into many European, Asian, and African languages and is the most widely used and most warmly praised catechism of the Reformation period.

The 1968 Synod of the Christian Reformed Church appointed a committee to prepare "a modern and accurate translation . . . which will serve as the official text of the Heidelberg Catechism and as a guide for catechism preaching." A translation was adopted by the Synod of 1975, and some editorial revisions were approved by the Synod of 1988.

The English translation follows the first German edition of the catechism except in two instances explained in footnotes to questions 57 and 80. The result of those inclusions is that the translation therefore actually follows the German text of the third edition as it was included in the Palatinate Church Order of November 15, 1563. This is the "received text" used throughout the world.

Biblical passages quoted in the catechism are taken from the New International Version. In the German editions, biblical quotations sometimes include additional words not found in the Greek text and therefore not included in recent translations such as the NIV. The additions from the German are indicated in footnotes in Q & A 4, 71, and 119.

LORD'S DAY 1

**1 Q. What is your only comfort
in life and in death?**

  A. That I am not my own,[1]
but belong—
    body and soul,
    in life and in death—[2]
to my faithful Savior Jesus Christ.[3]

    He has fully paid for all my sins with his precious blood,[4]
    and has set me free from the tyranny of the devil.[5]
    He also watches over me in such a way[6]
    that not a hair can fall from my head
    without the will of my Father in heaven:[7]
    in fact, all things must work together for my salvation.[8]

Because I belong to him,
Christ, by his Holy Spirit,
assures me of eternal life[9]
and makes me wholeheartedly willing and ready
from now on to live for him.[10]

[1] 1 Cor. 6:19–20
[2] Rom. 14:7–9
[3] 1 Cor. 3:23; Titus 2:14
[4] 1 Pet. 1:18–19; 1 John 1:7–9; 2:2
[5] John 8:34–36; Heb. 2:14–15; 1 John 3:1–11
[6] John 6:39–40; 10:27–30; 2 Thess. 3:3; 1 Pet. 1:5
[7] Matt. 10:29–31; Luke 21:16–18
[8] Rom. 8:28
[9] Rom. 8:15–16; 2 Cor. 1:21–22; 5:5; Eph. 1:13–14
[10] Rom. 8:1–17

**2 Q. What must you know
to live and die in the joy of this comfort?**

  A. Three things:
    first, how great my sin and misery are;[1]
    second, how I am set free from all my sins and misery;[2]
    third, how I am to thank God for such deliverance.[3]

[1] Rom. 3:9–10; 1 John 1:10
[2] John 17:3; Acts 4:12; 10:43
[3] Matt. 5:16; Rom. 6:13; Eph. 5:8–10; 2 Tim. 2:15; 1 Pet. 2:9–10

Part I: Misery

LORD'S DAY 2

3 Q. How do you come to know your misery?

   A. The law of God tells me.[1]

     [1] Rom. 3:20; 7:7–25

4 Q. What does God's law require of us?

   A. Christ teaches us this in summary in Matthew 22—

     Love the Lord your God
     with all your heart
     and with all your soul
     and with all your mind
     and with all your strength.[1]*
     This is the first and greatest commandment.

     And the second is like it:
     Love your neighbor as yourself.[2]

     All the Law and the Prophets hang
     on these two commandments.

     [1] Deut. 6:5
     [2] Lev. 19:18

5 Q. Can you live up to all this perfectly?

   A. No.[1]
     I have a natural tendency
     to hate God and my neighbor.[2]

     [1] Rom. 3:9–20, 23; 1 John 1:8, 10
     [2] Gen. 6:5; Jer. 17:9; Rom. 7:23–24; 8:7; Eph. 2:1–3; Titus 3:3

---

*Earlier and better manuscripts of Matthew 22 omit the words "and with all your strength." They are found in Mark 12:30.

LORD'S DAY 3

**6 Q. Did God create people
so wicked and perverse?**

A. No.
God created them good[1] and in his own image,[2]
that is, in true righteousness and holiness,[3]
so that they might
truly know God their creator,[4]
love him with all their heart,
and live with him in eternal happiness
for his praise and glory.[5]

[1] Gen. 1:31
[2] Gen. 1:26–27
[3] Eph. 4:24
[4] Col. 3:10
[5] Ps. 8

**7 Q. Then where does this corrupt human nature
come from?**

A. From the fall and disobedience of our first parents,
Adam and Eve, in Paradise.[1]
This fall has so poisoned our nature[2]
that we are born sinners—
corrupt from conception on.[3]

[1] Gen. 3
[2] Rom. 5:12, 18–19
[3] Ps. 51:5

**8 Q. But are we so corrupt
that we are totally unable to do any good
and inclined toward all evil?**

A. Yes,[1] unless we are born again,
by the Spirit of God.[2]

[1] Gen. 6:5; 8:21; Job 14:4; Isa. 53:6
[2] John 3:3–5

LORD'S DAY 4

**9 Q. But doesn't God do us an injustice
by requiring in his law
what we are unable to do?**

A. No, God created humans with the ability to keep the law.[1]
They, however, tempted by the devil,[2]
in reckless disobedience,[3]
robbed themselves and all their descendants of these gifts.[4]

[1] Gen. 1:31; Eph. 4:24
[2] Gen. 3:13; John 8:44
[3] Gen. 3:6
[4] Rom. 5:12, 18, 19

**10 Q. Will God permit
such disobedience and rebellion
to go unpunished?**

A. Certainly not.
He is terribly angry
about the sin we are born with
as well as the sins we personally commit.

As a just judge
he punishes them now and in eternity.[1]

He has declared:
"Cursed is everyone who does not continue to do
everything written in the Book of the Law."[2]

[1] Ex. 34:7; Ps. 5:4–6; Nah. 1:2; Rom. 1:18; Eph. 5:6; Heb. 9:27
[2] Gal. 3:10; Deut. 27:26

11 Q. But isn't God also merciful?

A. God is certainly merciful,[1]
but he is also just.[2]
His justice demands
that sin, committed against his supreme majesty,
be punished with the supreme penalty—
eternal punishment of body and soul.[3]

[1] Ex. 34:6–7; Ps. 103:8–9
[2] Ex. 34:7; Deut. 7:9–11; Ps. 5:4–6; Heb. 10:30–31
[3] Matt. 25:35–46

Part II: Deliverance

LORD'S DAY 5

**12 Q. According to God's righteous judgment
we deserve punishment
both in this world and forever after:
how then can we escape this punishment
and return to God's favor?**

A. God requires that his justice be satisfied.[1]
Therefore the claims of his justice
must be paid in full,
either by ourselves or another.[2]

[1] Ex. 23:7; Rom. 2:1–11
[2] Isa. 53:11; Rom. 8:3–4

13 Q. Can we pay this debt ourselves?

A. Certainly not.
Actually, we increase our guilt every day.[1]

[1] Matt. 6:12; Rom. 2:4–5

**14 Q. Can another creature—any at all—
pay this debt for us?**

A. No.
To begin with,
God will not punish another creature
for what a human is guilty of.[1]
Besides,
no mere creature can bear the weight
of God's eternal anger against sin
and release others from it.[2]

[1] Ezek. 18:4, 20; Heb. 2:14–18
[2] Ps. 49:7–9; 130:3

**15 Q. What kind of mediator and deliverer
should we look for then?**

A. One who is truly human[1] and truly righteous,[2]
yet more powerful than all creatures,
that is, one who is also true God.[3]

[1] Rom. 1:3; 1 Cor. 15:21; Heb. 2:17
[2] Isa. 53:9; 2 Cor. 5:21; Heb. 7:26
[3] Isa. 7:14; 9:6; Jer. 23:6; John 1:1

LORD'S DAY 6

**16 Q. Why must he be truly human
and truly righteous?**

A. God's justice demands
that human nature, which has sinned,
must pay for its sin;[1]
but a sinner could never pay for others.[2]

[1] Rom. 5:12, 15; 1 Cor. 15:21; Heb. 2:14–16
[2] Heb. 7:26–27; 1 Pet. 3:18

17 Q. Why must he also be true God?

A. So that,
by the power of his divinity,
he might bear the weight of God's anger in his humanity
and earn for us
and restore to us
righteousness and life.[1]

[1] Isa. 53; John 3:16; 2 Cor. 5:21

**18 Q. And who is this mediator—
true God and at the same time
truly human and truly righteous?**

A. Our Lord Jesus Christ,[1]
who was given us
to set us completely free
and to make us right with God.[2]

[1] Matt. 1:21–23; Luke 2:11; 1 Tim. 2:5
[2] 1 Cor. 1:30

19 Q. How do you come to know this?

A. The holy gospel tells me.
God himself began to reveal the gospel already in Paradise;
later, he proclaimed it
by the holy patriarchs[2] and prophets,[3]
and portrayed it
by the sacrifices and other ceremonies of the law;[4]
finally, he fulfilled it
through his own dear Son.[5]

[1] Gen. 3:15
[2] Gen. 22:18; 49:10
[3] Isa. 53; Jer. 23:5–6; Mic. 7:18–20; Acts 10:43; Heb. 1:1–2
[4] Lev. 1–7; John 5:46; Heb. 10:1–10
[5] Rom. 10:4; Gal. 4:4–5; Col. 2:17

LORD'S DAY 7

**20 Q. Are all saved through Christ
just as all were lost through Adam?**

A. No.
Only those are saved
who by true faith
    are grafted into Christ
    and accept all his blessings.[1]

[1] Matt. 7:14; John 3:16, 18, 36; Rom. 11:16–21

21 Q. What is true faith?

A. True faith is
    not only a knowledge and conviction
        that everything God reveals in his Word is true;[1]
    it is also a deep-rooted assurance,[2]
        created in me by the Holy Spirit[3] through the gospel,[4]
        that, out of sheer grace earned for us by Christ,[5]
            not only others, but I too,[6]
                have had my sins forgiven,
                have been made forever right with God,
                and have been granted salvation.[7]

[1] John 17:3, 17; Heb. 11:1–3; James 2:19
[2] Rom. 4:18–21; 5:1; 10:10; Heb. 4:14–16
[3] Matt. 16:15–17; John 3:5; Acts 16:14
[4] Rom. 1:16; 10:17; 1 Cor. 1:21
[5] Rom. 3:21–26; Gal. 2:16; Eph. 2:8–10
[6] Gal. 2:20
[7] Rom. 1:17; Heb. 10:10

22 Q. What then must a Christian believe?

A. Everything God promises us in the gospel.[1]
    That gospel is summarized for us
    in the articles of our Christian faith—
    a creed beyond doubt,
    and confessed throughout the world.

[1] Matt. 28:18–20; John 20:30–31

23 Q. What are these articles?

A. I believe in God, the Father almighty,
    creator of heaven and earth.

I believe in Jesus Christ, his only Son, our Lord,
    who was conceived by the Holy Spirit
    and born of the virgin Mary.
    He suffered under Pontius Pilate,
    was crucified, died, and was buried;
    he descended to hell.
    The third day he rose again from the dead.
    He ascended to heaven
    and is seated at the right hand of God the Father almighty.
    From there he will come to judge the living and the dead.

I believe in the Holy Spirit,
    the holy catholic church,
    the communion of saints,
    the forgiveness of sins,
    the resurrection of the body,
    and the life everlasting. Amen.

LORD'S DAY 8

24 Q. How are these articles divided?

   A. Into three parts:
      God the Father and our creation;
      God the Son and our deliverance;
      God the Holy Spirit and our sanctification.

**25 Q. Since there is but one God,[1]
why do you speak of three:
Father, Son, and Holy Spirit?**

   A. Because that is how
      God has revealed himself in his Word:[2]
      these three distinct persons
      are one, true, eternal God.

[1] Deut. 6:4; 1 Cor. 8:4, 6
[2] Matt. 3:16–17; 28:18–19; Luke 4:18 (Isa. 61:1); John 14:26; 15:26; 2 Cor. 13:14;
Gal. 4:6; Tit. 3:5–6

God the Father

LORD'S DAY 9

**26 Q. What do you believe when you say,
"I believe in God, the Father almighty,
creator of heaven and earth"?**

A. That the eternal Father of our Lord Jesus Christ,
who out of nothing created heaven and earth
and everything in them,[1]
who still upholds and rules them
by his eternal counsel and providence,[2]
is my God and Father
because of Christ his Son.[3]

I trust him so much that I do not doubt
he will provide
whatever I need
for body and soul,[4]
and he will turn to my good
whatever adversity he sends me
in this sad world.[5]

He is able to do this because he is almighty God;[6]
he desires to do this because he is a faithful Father.[7]

[1] Gen. 1 & 2; Ex. 20:11; Ps. 33:6; Isa. 44:24; Acts 4:24; 14:15
[2] Ps. 104; Matt. 6:30; 10:29; Eph. 1:11
[3] John 1:12–13; Rom. 8:15–16; Gal. 4:4–7; Eph. 1:5
[4] Ps. 55:22; Matt. 6:25–26; Luke 12:22–31
[5] Rom. 8:28
[6] Gen. 18:14; Rom. 8:31–39
[7] Matt. 7:9–11

LORD'S DAY 10

**27 Q. What do you understand
by the providence of God?**

    A. Providence is
        the almighty and ever present power of God[1]
        by which he upholds, as with his hand,
            heaven
            and earth
            and all creatures,[2]
        and so rules them that
            leaf and blade,
            rain and drought,
            fruitful and lean years,
            food and drink,
            health and sickness,
            prosperity and poverty—[3]
        all things, in fact, come to us
            not by chance[4]
            but from his fatherly hand.[5]

[1] Jer. 23:23–24; Acts 17:24–28
[2] Heb. 1:3
[3] Jer. 5:24; Acts 14:15–17; John 9:3; Prov. 22:2
[4] Prov. 16:33
[5] Matt. 10:29

**28 Q. How does the knowledge
of God's creation and providence
help us?**

    A. We can be patient when things go against us,[1]
        thankful when things go well,[2]
        and for the future we can have
        good confidence in our faithful God and Father
        that nothing will separate us from his love.[3]
        All creatures are so completely in his hand
            that without his will
            they can neither move nor be moved.[4]

[1] Job 1:21–22; James 1:3
[2] Deut. 8:10; 1 Thess. 5:18
[3] Ps. 55:22; Rom. 5:3–5; 8:38–39
[4] Job 1:12; 2:6; Prov. 21:1; Acts 17:24–28

God the Son

LORD'S DAY 11

**29 Q. Why is the Son of God called "Jesus,"
meaning "savior"?**

A. Because he saves us from our sins.[1]
Salvation cannot be found in anyone else;
it is futile to look for any salvation elsewhere.[2]

[1] Matt. 1:21; Heb. 7:25
[2] Isa. 43:11; John 15:5; Acts 4:11–12; 1 Tim. 2:5

**30 Q. Do those who look for
their salvation and security
in saints, in themselves, or elsewhere
really believe in the only savior Jesus?**

A. No.
Although they boast of being his,
by their deeds they deny
the only savior and deliverer, Jesus.[1]

Either Jesus is not a perfect savior,
or those who in true faith accept this savior
have in him all they need for their salvation.[2]

[1] 1 Cor. 1:12–13; Gal. 5:4
[2] Col. 1:19–20; 2:10; 1 John 1:7

LORD'S DAY 12

**31 Q. Why is he called "Christ,"
meaning "anointed"?**

A. Because he has been ordained by God the Father
and has been anointed with the Holy Spirit[1]
to be
our chief prophet and teacher[2]
who perfectly reveals to us
the secret counsel and will of God for our deliverance;[3]
our only high priest[4]
who has set us free by the one sacrifice of his body,[5]
and who continually pleads our cause with the Father;[6]
and our eternal king[7]
who governs us by his Word and Spirit,
and who guards us and keeps us
in the freedom he has won for us.[8]

[1] Luke 3:21–22; 4:14–19 (Isa. 61:1); Heb. 1:9 (Ps. 45:7)
[2] Acts 3:22 (Deut. 18:15)
[3] John 1:18; 15:15
[4] Heb. 7:17 (Ps. 110:4)
[5] Heb. 9:12; 10:11–14
[6] Rom. 8:34; Heb. 9:24
[7] Matt. 21:5 (Zech. 9:9)
[8] Matt. 28:18–20; John 10:28; Rev. 12:10–11

32 Q. But why are you called a Christian?

A. Because by faith I am a member of Christ[1]
and so I share in his anointing.[2]
I am anointed
to confess his name,[3]
to present myself to him as a living sacrifice of thanks,[4]
to strive with a good conscience against sin and the devil
in this life,[5]
and afterward to reign with Christ
over all creation
for all eternity.[6]

[1] 1 Cor. 12:12–27
[2] Acts 2:17 (Joel 2:28); 1 John 2:27
[3] Matt. 10:32; Rom. 10:9–10; Heb. 13:15
[4] Rom. 12:1; 1 Pet. 2:5, 9
[5] Gal. 5:16–17; Eph. 6:11; 1 Tim. 1:18–19
[6] Matt. 25:34; 2 Tim. 2:12

LORD'S DAY 13

**33 Q. Why is he called God's "only Son"
when we also are God's children?**

A. Because Christ alone is the eternal, natural Son of God.[1]
We, however, are adopted children of God—
adopted by grace through Christ.[2]

[1] John 1:1–3, 14, 18; Heb. 1
[2] John 1:12; Rom. 8:14–17; Eph. 1:5–6

34 Q. Why do you call him "our Lord"?

A. Because—
not with gold or silver,
but with his precious blood—[1]
he has set us free
from sin and from the tyranny of the devil,[2]
and has bought us,
body and soul,
to be his very own.[3]

[1] 1 Pet. 1:18–19
[2] Col. 1:13–14; Heb. 2:14–15
[3] 1 Cor. 6:20; 1 Tim. 2:5–6

LORD'S DAY 14

**35 Q. What does it mean that he
"was conceived by the Holy Spirit
and born of the virgin Mary"?**

A. That the eternal Son of God,
who is and remains
true and eternal God,[1]
took to himself,
through the working of the Holy Spirit,[2]
from the flesh and blood of the virgin Mary,[3]
a truly human nature
so that he might become David's true descendant,[4]
like his brothers in every way[5]
except for sin.[6]

[1] John 1:1; 10:30–36; Acts 13:33 (Ps. 2:7); Col. 1:15–17; 1 John 5:20
[2] Luke 1:35
[3] Matt. 1:18–23; John 1:14; Gal. 4:4; Heb. 2:14
[4] 2 Sam. 7:12–16; Ps. 132:11; Matt. 1:1; Rom. 1:3
[5] Phil. 2:7; Heb. 2:17
[6] Heb. 4:15; 7:26–27

**36 Q. How does the holy conception and birth of Christ
benefit you?**

A. He is our mediator,[1]
and with his innocence and perfect holiness
he removes from God's sight
my sin—mine since I was conceived.[2]

[1] 1 Tim. 2:5–6; Heb. 9:13–15
[2] Rom. 8:3–4; 2 Cor. 5:21; Gal. 4:4–5; 1 Pet. 1:18–19

LORD'S DAY 15

**37 Q. What do you understand
by the word "suffered"?**

A. That during his whole life on earth,
but especially at the end,
Christ sustained
in body and soul
the anger of God against the sin of the whole human race.[1]

This he did in order that,
by his suffering as the only atoning sacrifice,[2]
he might set us free, body and soul,
from eternal condemnation,[3]
and gain for us
God's grace,
righteousness,
and eternal life.[4]

[1] Isa. 53; 1 Pet. 2:24; 3:18
[2] Rom. 3:25; Heb. 10:14; 1 John 2:2; 4:10
[3] Rom. 8:1–4; Gal. 3:13
[4] John 3:16; Rom. 3:24–26

**38 Q. Why did he suffer
"under Pontius Pilate" as judge?**

A. So that he,
though innocent,
might be condemned by a civil judge,[1]
and so free us from the severe judgment of God
that was to fall on us.[2]

[1] Luke 23:13–24; John 19:4, 12–16
[2] Isa. 53:4–5; 2 Cor. 5:21; Gal. 3:13

**39 Q. Is it significant
that he was "crucified"
instead of dying some other way?**

A. Yes.
This death convinces me
that he shouldered the curse
which lay on me,
since death by crucifixion was accursed by God.[1]

[1] Gal. 3:10–13 (Deut. 21:23)

LORD'S DAY 16

40 Q. Why did Christ have to go all the way to death?

A. Because God's justice and truth demand it:[1]
only the death of God's Son could pay for our sin.[2]

[1] Gen. 2:17
[2] Rom. 8:3–4; Phil. 2:8; Heb. 2:9

41 Q. Why was he "buried"?

A. His burial testifies
that he really died.[1]

[1] Isa. 53:9; John 19:38–42; Acts 13:29; 1 Cor. 15:3–4

**42 Q. Since Christ has died for us,
why do we still have to die?**

A. Our death does not pay the debt of our sins.[1]
Rather, it puts an end to our sinning
and is our entrance into eternal life.[2]

[1] Ps. 49:7
[2] John 5:24; Phil. 1:21–23; 1 Thess. 5:9–10

**43 Q. What further advantage do we receive
from Christ's sacrifice and death on the cross?**

A. Through Christ's death
our old selves are crucified, put to death, and buried with him,[1]
so that the evil desires of the flesh
may no longer rule us,[2]
but that instead we may dedicate ourselves
as an offering of gratitude to him.[3]

[1] Rom. 6:5–11; Col. 2:11–12
[2] Rom. 6:12–14
[3] Rom. 12:1; Eph. 5:1–2

**44 Q. Why does the creed add,
"He descended to hell"?**

A. To assure me in times of personal crisis and temptation
that Christ my Lord,
by suffering unspeakable anguish, pain, and terror of soul,
especially on the cross but also earlier,
has delivered me from the anguish and torment of hell.[1]

[1] Isa. 53; Matt. 26:36–46; 27:45–46; Luke 22:44; Heb. 5:7–10

LORD'S DAY 17

**45 Q. How does Christ's resurrection
     benefit us?**

   A. First, by his resurrection he has overcome death,
       so that he might make us share in the righteousness
       he won for us by his death.[1]

   Second, by his power we too
   are already now resurrected to a new life.[2]

   Third, Christ's resurrection
   is a guarantee of our glorious resurrection.[3]

[1] Rom. 4:25; 1 Cor. 15:16–20; 1 Pet. 1:3–5
[2] Rom. 6:5–11; Eph. 2:4–6; Col. 3:1–4
[3] Rom. 8:11; 1 Cor. 15:12–23; Phil. 3:20–21

LORD'S DAY 18

**46 Q. What do you mean by saying,
"He ascended to heaven"?**

A. That Christ,
   while his disciples watched,
was lifted up from the earth to heaven[1]
and will be there for our good[2]
until he comes again
   to judge the living and the dead.[3]

[1] Luke 24:50–51; Acts 1:9–11
[2] Rom. 8:34; Eph. 4:8–10; Heb. 7:23–25; 9:24
[3] Acts 1:11

**47 Q. But isn't Christ with us
until the end of the world
as he promised us?[1]**

A. Christ is truly human and truly God.
   In his human nature Christ is not now on earth;[2]
   but in his divinity, majesty, grace, and Spirit
   he is not absent from us for a moment.[3]

[1] Matt. 28:20
[2] Acts 1:9–11; 3:19–21
[3] Matt. 28:18–20; John 14:16–19

**48 Q. If his humanity is not present
wherever his divinity is,
then aren't the two natures of Christ
separated from each other?**

A. Certainly not.
Since divinity
   is not limited
   and is present everywhere,[1]
it is evident that
   Christ's divinity is surely beyond the bounds of
      the humanity he has taken on,
   but at the same time his divinity is in
   and remains personally united to
      his humanity.[2]

[1] Jer. 23:23–24; Acts 7:48–49 (Isa. 66:1)
[2] John 1:14; 3:13; Col. 2:9

49 Q. How does Christ's ascension to heaven benefit us?

A. First, he pleads our cause
in heaven
in the presence of his Father.[1]

Second, we have our own flesh in heaven—
a guarantee that Christ our head
will take us, his members,
to himself in heaven.[2]

Third, he sends his Spirit to us on earth
as a further guarantee.[3]
By the Spirit's power
we make the goal of our lives,
not earthly things,
but the things above where Christ is,
sitting at God's right hand.[4]

[1] Rom. 8:34; 1 John 2:1
[2] John 14:2; 17:24; Eph. 2:4–6
[3] John 14:16; 2 Cor. 1:21–22; 5:5
[4] Col. 3:1–4

LORD'S DAY 19

**50 Q. Why the next words:
"and is seated at the right hand of God"?**

   A. Christ ascended to heaven,
      there to show that he is head of his church,[1]
         and that the Father rules all things through him.[2]

      [1] Eph. 1:20–23; Col. 1:18
      [2] Matt. 28:18; John 5:22–23

**51 Q. How does this glory of Christ our head
benefit us?**

   A. First, through his Holy Spirit
      he pours out his gifts from heaven
         upon us his members.[1]

      Second, by his power
         he defends us and keeps us safe
         from all enemies.[2]

      [1] Acts 2:33; Eph. 4:7–12
      [2] Ps. 110:1–2; John 10:27–30; Rev. 19:11–16

**52 Q. How does Christ's return
"to judge the living and the dead"
comfort you?**

   A. In all my distress and persecution
      I turn my eyes to the heavens
      and confidently await as judge the very One
         who has already stood trial in my place before God
         and so has removed the whole curse from me.[1]
      All his enemies and mine
         he will condemn to everlasting punishment:
      but me and all his chosen ones
         he will take along with him
         into the joy and the glory of heaven.[2]

      [1] Luke 21:28; Rom. 8:22–25; Phil. 3:20–21; Tit. 2:13–14
      [2] Matt. 25:31–46; 2 Thess. 1:6–10

God the Holy Spirit

LORD'S DAY 20

**53 Q. What do you believe
concerning "the Holy Spirit"?**

A. First, he, as well as the Father and the Son,
is eternal God.[1]

Second, he has been given to me personally,[2]
so that, by true faith,
he makes me share in Christ and all his blessings,[3]
comforts me,[4]
and remains with me forever.[5]

[1] Gen. 1:1–2; Matt. 28:19; Acts 5:3–4
[2] 1 Cor. 6:19; 2 Cor. 1:21–22; Gal. 4:6
[3] Gal. 3:14
[4] John 15:26; Acts 9:31
[5] John 14:16–17; 1 Pet. 4:14

LORD'S DAY 21

**54 Q. What do you believe
concerning "the holy catholic church"?**

A. I believe that the Son of God
   through his Spirit and Word,[1]
   out of the entire human race,[2]
   from the beginning of the world to its end,[3]
gathers, protects, and preserves for himself
   a community chosen for eternal life[4]
      and united in true faith.[5]
And of this community I am[6] and always will be[7]
   a living member.

[1] John 10:14–16; Acts 20:28; Rom. 10:14–17; Col. 1:18
[2] Gen. 26:3b–4; Rev. 5:9
[3] Isa. 59:21; 1 Cor. 11:26
[4] Matt. 16:18; John 10:28–30; Rom. 8:28–30; Eph. 1:3–14
[5] Acts 2:42–47; Eph. 4:1–6
[6] 1 John 3:14, 19–21
[7] John 10:27–28; 1 Cor. 1:4–9; 1 Pet. 1:3–5

**55 Q. What do you understand by
"the communion of saints"?**

A. First, that believers one and all,
as members of this community,
share in Christ
and in all his treasures and gifts.[1]

Second, that each member
should consider it a duty
to use these gifts
   readily and cheerfully
   for the service and enrichment
   of the other members.[2]

[1] Rom. 8:32; 1 Cor. 6:17; 12:4–7, 12–13; 1 John 1:3
[2] Rom. 12:4–8; 1 Cor. 12:20–27; 13:1–7; Phil. 2:4–8

**56 Q. What do you believe
concerning "the forgiveness of sins"?**

A. I believe that God,
　　　because of Christ's atonement,
　　will never hold against me
　　　any of my sins[1]
　　　nor my sinful nature
　　　　which I need to struggle against all my life.[2]

Rather, in his grace
　　God grants me the righteousness of Christ
　　to free me forever from judgment.[3]

[1] Ps. 103:3–4, 10, 12; Mic. 7:18–19; 2 Cor. 5:18–21; 1 John 1:7; 2:2
[2] Rom. 7:21–25
[3] John 3:17–18; Rom. 8:1–2

LORD'S DAY 22

**57 Q. How does "the resurrection of the body"
comfort you?**

A. Not only my soul
    will be taken immediately after this life
    to Christ its head,[1]
but even my very flesh, raised by the power of Christ,
    will be reunited with my soul
    and made like Christ's glorious* body.[2]

[1] Luke 23:43; Phil. 1:21–23
[2] 1 Cor. 15:20, 42–46, 54; Phil. 3:21; 1 John 3:2

**58 Q. How does the article
concerning "life everlasting"
comfort you?**

A. Even as I already now
    experience in my heart
    the beginning of eternal joy,[1]
so after this life I will have
    perfect blessedness such as
        no eye has seen,
        no ear has heard,
        no human heart has ever imagined:
a blessedness in which to praise God eternally.[2]

[1] Rom. 14:17
[2] John 17:3; 1 Cor. 2:9

*The first edition had here the German word for "holy." This was later corrected to the German word for "glorious."

LORD'S DAY 23

59 Q. What good does it do you, however, to believe all this?

A. In Christ I am right with God
and heir to life everlasting.[1]

[1] John 3:36; Rom. 1:17 (Hab. 2:4); Rom. 5:1-2

60 Q. How are you right with God?

A. Only by true faith in Jesus Christ.[1]

Even though my conscience accuses me
of having grievously sinned against all God's commandments
and of never having kept any of them,[2]
and even though I am still inclined toward all evil,[3]
nevertheless,
without my deserving it at all,[4]
out of sheer grace,[5]
God grants and credits to me
the perfect satisfaction, righteousness, and holiness of Christ,[6]
as if I had never sinned nor been a sinner,
as if I had been as perfectly obedient
as Christ was obedient for me.[7]

All I need to do
is to accept this gift of God with a believing heart.[8]

[1] Rom. 3:21-28; Gal. 2:16; Eph. 2:8-9; Phil 3:8-11
[2] Rom. 3:9-10
[3] Rom. 7:23
[4] Tit. 3:4-5
[5] Rom. 3:24; Eph. 2:8
[6] Rom. 4:3-5 (Gen. 15:6); 2 Cor. 5:17-19; 1 John 2:1-2
[7] Rom. 4:24-25; 2 Cor. 5:21
[8] John 3:18; Acts 16:30-31

**61 Q. Why do you say that
by faith alone
you are right with God?**

A. It is not because of any value my faith has
that God is pleased with me.
Only Christ's satisfaction, righteousness, and holiness
make me right with God.[1]
And I can receive this righteousness and make it mine
in no other way than
by faith alone.[2]

[1] 1 Cor. 1:30–31
[2] Rom. 10:10; 1 John 5:10–12

LORD'S DAY 24

62 Q. Why can't the good we do
make us right with God,
or at least help make us right with him?

    A. Because the righteousness
which can pass God's scrutiny
    must be entirely perfect
    and must in every way measure up to the divine law.[1]
Even the very best we do in this life
    is imperfect
    and stained with sin.[2]

    [1] Rom. 3:20; Gal. 3:10 (Deut. 27:26)
    [2] Isa. 64:6

63 Q. How can you say that the good we do
doesn't earn anything
when God promises to reward it
in this life and the next?[1]

    A. This reward is not earned;
it is a gift of grace.[2]

    [1] Matt. 5:12; Heb. 11:6
    [2] Luke 17:10; 2 Tim. 4:7–8

64 Q. But doesn't this teaching
make people indifferent and wicked?

    A. No.
It is impossible
    for those grafted into Christ by true faith
not to produce fruits of gratitude.[1]

    [1] Luke 6:43–45; John 15:5

The Sacraments

LORD'S DAY 25

**65 Q. It is by faith alone
that we share in Christ and all his blessings:
where then does that faith come from?**

A. The Holy Spirit produces it in our hearts[1]
by the preaching of the holy gospel,[2]
and confirms it
through our use of the holy sacraments.[3]

[1] John 3:5; 1 Cor. 2:10–14; Eph. 2:8
[2] Rom. 10:17; 1 Pet. 1:23–25
[3] Matt. 28:19–20; 1 Cor. 10:16

66 Q. What are sacraments?

A. Sacraments are holy signs and seals for us to see.
They were instituted by God so that
by our use of them
he might make us understand more clearly
the promise of the gospel,
and might put his seal on that promise.[1]

And this is God's gospel promise:
to forgive our sins and give us eternal life
by grace alone
because of Christ's one sacrifice
finished on the cross.[2]

[1] Gen. 17:11; Deut. 30:6; Rom. 4:11
[2] Matt. 26:27–28; Acts 2:38; Heb. 10:10

**67 Q. Are both the word and the sacraments then
intended to focus our faith
on the sacrifice of Jesus Christ on the cross
as the only ground of our salvation?**

A. Right!
In the gospel the Holy Spirit teaches us
and through the holy sacraments he assures us
that our entire salvation
rests on Christ's one sacrifice for us on the cross.[1]

[1] Rom. 6:3; 1 Cor. 11:26; Gal. 3:27

**68 Q. How many sacraments
did Christ institute in the New Testament?**

A. Two: baptism and the Lord's Supper.[1]

[1] Matt. 28:19–20; 1 Cor. 11:23–26

Baptism

LORD'S DAY 26

**69 Q. How does baptism
remind you and assure you
that Christ's one sacrifice on the cross
is for you personally?**

A. In this way:
Christ instituted this outward washing[1]
and with it gave the promise that,
   as surely as water washes away the dirt from the body,
   so certainly his blood and his Spirit
   wash away my soul's impurity,
      in other words, all my sins.[2]

[1] Acts 2:38
[2] Matt. 3:11; Rom. 6:3–10; 1 Pet. 3:21

**70 Q. What does it mean
to be washed with Christ's blood and Spirit?**

A. To be washed with Christ's blood means
   that God, by grace, has forgiven my sins
      because of Christ's blood
      poured out for me in his sacrifice on the cross.[1]

To be washed with Christ's Spirit means
   that the Holy Spirit has renewed me
   and set me apart to be a member of Christ
      so that more and more I become dead to sin
      and increasingly live a holy and blameless life.[2]

[1] Zech. 13:1; Eph. 1:7–8; Heb. 12:24; 1 Pet. 1:2; Rev. 1:5
[2] Ezek. 36:25–27; John 3:5–8; Rom. 6:4; 1 Cor. 6:11; Col. 2:11–12

**71 Q. Where does Christ promise
that we are washed with his blood and Spirit
as surely as we are washed
with the water of baptism?**

  A. In the institution of baptism where he says:

> "Therefore go and make disciples of all nations,
> baptizing them in the name of the Father
> and of the Son
> and of the Holy Spirit."[1]

> "Whoever believes and is baptized will be saved,
> but whoever does not believe will be condemned."[2]*

> This promise is repeated when Scripture calls baptism
> the washing of rebirth[3] and
> the washing away of sins.[4]

[1] Matt. 28:19
[2] Mark 16:16
[3] Tit. 3:5
[4] Acts 22:16

LORD'S DAY 27

**72 Q. Does this outward washing with water
itself wash away sins?**

A. No, only Jesus Christ's blood and the Holy Spirit
   cleanse us from all sins.[1]

   [1] Matt. 3:11; 1 Pet. 3:21; 1 John 1:7

**73 Q. Why then does the Holy Spirit call baptism
the washing of rebirth and
the washing away of sins?**

A. God has good reason for these words.
   He wants to teach us that
      the blood and Spirit of Christ wash away our sins
      just as water washes away dirt from our bodies.[1]

   But more important,
   he wants to assure us, by this divine pledge and sign,
      that the washing away of our sins spiritually
      is as real as physical washing with water.[2]

   [1] 1 Cor. 6:11; Rev. 1:5; 7:14
   [2] Acts 2:38; Rom. 6:3–4; Gal. 3:27

74 Q. Should infants, too, be baptized?

A. Yes.
   Infants as well as adults
      are in God's covenant and are his people.[1]
   They, no less than adults, are promised
      the forgiveness of sin through Christ's blood
      and the Holy Spirit who produces faith.[2]

   Therefore, by baptism, the mark of the covenant,
      infants should be received into the Christian church
      and should be distinguished from the children
         of unbelievers.[3]
   This was done in the Old Testament by circumcision,[4]
      which was replaced in the New Testament by baptism.[5]

   [1] Gen. 17:7; Matt. 19:14
   [2] Isa. 44:1–3; Acts 2:38–39; 16:31
   [3] Acts 10:47; 1 Cor. 7:14
   [4] Gen. 17:9–14
   [5] Col. 2:11–13

The Lord's Supper

LORD'S DAY 28

**75 Q. How does the Lord's Supper
remind you and assure you
that you share in
Christ's one sacrifice on the cross
and in all his gifts?**

  A. In this way:
  Christ has commanded me and all believers
  to eat this broken bread and to drink this cup.
  With this command he gave this promise:[1]

  First,
      as surely as I see with my eyes
          the bread of the Lord broken for me
          and the cup given to me,
      so surely
          his body was offered and broken for me
          and his blood poured out for me
              on the cross.

  Second,
      as surely as
          I receive from the hand of the one who serves,
          and taste with my mouth
              the bread and cup of the Lord,
              given me as sure signs of Christ's body and blood,
      so surely
          he nourishes and refreshes my soul for eternal life
          with his crucified body and poured-out blood.

[1] Matt. 26:26–28; Mark 14:22–24; Luke 22:19–20; 1 Cor. 11:23–25

**76 Q. What does it mean
to eat the crucified body of Christ
and to drink his poured-out blood?**

A. It means
to accept with a believing heart
the entire suffering and death of Christ
and by believing
to receive forgiveness of sins and eternal life.[1]

But it means more.
Through the Holy Spirit, who lives both in Christ and in us,
we are united more and more to Christ's blessed body.[2]
And so, although he is in heaven[3] and we are on earth,
we are flesh of his flesh and bone of his bone.[4]
And we forever live on and are governed by one Spirit,
as members of our body are by one soul.[5]

[1] John 6:35, 40, 50–54
[2] John 6:55–56; 1 Cor. 12:13
[3] Acts 1:9–11; 1 Cor. 11:26; Col. 3:1
[4] 1 Cor. 6:15–17; Eph. 5:29–30; 1 John 4:13
[5] John 6:56–58; 15:1–6; Eph. 4:15–16; 1 John 3:24

77 Q. Where does Christ promise
to nourish and refresh believers
with his body and blood
as surely as
they eat this broken bread
and drink this cup?

  A. In the institution of the Lord's Supper:

  "The Lord Jesus, on the night he was betrayed,
  took bread, and when he had given thanks,
  he broke it and said,
    'This is my body, which is for you;
    do this in remembrance of me.'
  In the same way, after supper he took the cup, saying,
    'This cup is the new covenant in my blood;
    do this, whenever you drink it,
    in remembrance of me.'
  For whenever you eat this bread and drink this cup,
  you proclaim the Lord's death
  until he comes."[1]

This promise is repeated by Paul in these words:

  "Is not the cup of thanksgiving for which we give thanks
    a participation in the blood of Christ?
  And is not the bread that we break
    a participation in the body of Christ?
  Because there is one loaf, we, who are many, are one body,
  for we all partake of the one loaf."[2]

[1] 1 Cor. 11:23–26
[2] 1 Cor. 10:16–17

LORD'S DAY 29

**78 Q. Are the bread and wine changed into
the real body and blood of Christ?**

A. No.
Just as the water of baptism
is not changed into Christ's blood
and does not itself wash away sins
but is simply God's sign and assurance,[1]
so too the bread of the Lord's Supper
is not changed into the actual body of Christ[2]
even though it is called the body of Christ[3]
in keeping with the nature and language of sacraments.[4]

[1] Eph. 5:26; Tit. 3:5
[2] Matt. 26:26–29
[3] 1 Cor. 10:16–17; 11:26–28
[4] Gen. 17:10–11; Ex. 12:11, 13; 1 Cor. 10:1–4

**79 Q. Why then does Christ call
the bread his body
and the cup his blood,
or the new covenant in his blood?
(Paul uses the words,
a participation in Christ's body and blood.)**

A. Christ has good reason for these words.
He wants to teach us that
as bread and wine nourish our temporal life,
so too his crucified body and poured-out blood
truly nourish our souls for eternal life.[1]

But more important,
he wants to assure us, by this visible sign and pledge,
that we, through the Holy Spirit's work,
share in his true body and blood
as surely as our mouths
receive these holy signs in his remembrance,[2]
and that all of his suffering and obedience
are as definitely ours
as if we personally
had suffered and paid for our sins.[3]

[1] John 6:51, 55
[2] 1 Cor. 10:16–17; 11:26
[3] Rom. 6:5–11

LORD'S DAY 30

***80 Q. How does the Lord's Supper
    differ from the Roman Catholic Mass?**

A.   The Lord's Supper declares to us
        that our sins have been completely forgiven
        through the one sacrifice of Jesus Christ
        which he himself finished on the cross once for all.[1]
    It also declares to us
        that the Holy Spirit grafts us into Christ,[2]
        who with his very body
        is now in heaven at the right hand of the Father[3]
        where he wants us to worship him.[4]

[But the Mass teaches
        that the living and the dead
        do not have their sins forgiven
        through the suffering of Christ
        unless Christ is still offered for them daily by the priests.
    It also teaches
        that Christ is bodily present
        in the form of bread and wine
        where Christ is therefore to be worshiped.
    Thus the Mass is basically
        nothing but a denial
        of the one sacrifice and suffering of Jesus Christ
        and a condemnable idolatry.]

[1] John 19:30; Heb. 7:27; 9:12, 25-26; 10:10-18
[2] 1 Cor. 6:17; 10:16-17
[3] Acts 7:55-56; Heb. 1:3; 8:1
[4] Matt. 6:20-21; John 4:21-24; Phil. 3:20; Col. 3:1-3

*Q&A 80 was altogether absent from the first German edition of the Heidelberg Catechism (January 1563) but appeared in a shorter form in the second German edition (March 1563). The translation above is of the expanded text of the third German edition (ca. April 1563). Its strong tone reflects the setting in which the catechism was written.

In response to a mandate from Synod 1998, the Christian Reformed Church's Interchurch Relations Committee conducted a study of Q&A 80 and the Roman Catholic Mass. Based on this study, Synod 2004 declared that "Q&A 80 can no longer be held in its current form as part of our confession." Synod 2006 directed that Q&A 80 remain in the CRC's text of the Heidelberg Catechism but that the last three paragraphs be placed in brackets to indicate that they do not accurately reflect the official teaching and practice of today's Roman Catholic Church and are no longer confessionally binding on members of the CRC.

**81 Q. Who are to come
to the Lord's table?**

A. Those who are displeased with themselves
because of their sins,
but who nevertheless trust
that their sins are pardoned
and that their continuing weakness is covered
by the suffering and death of Christ,
and who also desire more and more
to strengthen their faith
and to lead a better life.

Hypocrites and those who are unrepentant, however,
eat and drink judgment on themselves.[1]

[1] 1 Cor. 10:19–22; 11:26–32

**82 Q. Are those to be admitted
to the Lord's Supper
who show by what they say and do
that they are unbelieving and ungodly?**

A. No, that would dishonor God's covenant
and bring down God's anger upon the entire congregation.[1]
Therefore, according to the instruction of Christ
and his apostles,
the Christian church is duty-bound to exclude such people,
by the official use of the keys of the kingdom,
until they reform their lives.

[1] 1 Cor. 11:17–32; Ps. 50:14–16; Isa. 1:11–17

LORD'S DAY 31

83 Q. What are the keys of the kingdom?

  A. The preaching of the holy gospel
and Christian discipline toward repentance.
Both preaching and discipline
    open the kingdom of heaven to believers
    and close it to unbelievers.[1]

  [1] Matt. 16:19; John 20:22–23

**84 Q. How does preaching the gospel
open and close the kingdom of heaven?**

  A. According to the command of Christ:

The kingdom of heaven is opened
by proclaiming and publicly declaring
    to all believers, each and every one, that,
    as often as they accept the gospel promise in true faith,
    God, because of what Christ has done,
    truly forgives all their sins.

The kingdom of heaven is closed, however,
by proclaiming and publicly declaring
    to unbelievers and hypocrites that,
    as long as they do not repent,
    the anger of God and eternal condemnation
    rest on them.

God's judgment, both in this life and in the life to come,
    is based on this gospel testimony.[1]

  [1] Matt. 16:19; John 3:31–36; 20:21–23

**85 Q. How is the kingdom of heaven
closed and opened by Christian discipline?**

A. According to the command of Christ:

Those who, though called Christians,
    profess unchristian teachings or live unchristian lives,
and after repeated and loving counsel
    refuse to abandon their errors and wickedness,
and after being reported to the church, that is, to its officers,
    fail to respond also to their admonition—
such persons the officers exclude
    from the Christian fellowship
by withholding the sacraments from them,
and God himself excludes them from the kingdom of Christ.[1]

Such persons,
    when promising and demonstrating genuine reform,
are received again
    as members of Christ
    and of his church.[2]

[1] Matt. 18:15–20; 1 Cor. 5:3–5, 11–13; 2 Thess. 3:14–15
[2] Luke 15:20–24; 2 Cor. 2:6–11

Part III: Gratitude

LORD'S DAY 32

**86 Q. We have been delivered
from our misery
by God's grace alone through Christ
and not because we have earned it:
why then must we still do good?**

A. To be sure, Christ has redeemed us by his blood.
But we do good because
Christ by his Spirit is also renewing us to be like himself,
so that in all our living
we may show that we are thankful to God
for all he has done for us,[1]
and so that he may be praised through us.[2]

And we do good
so that we may be assured of our faith by its fruits,[3]
and so that by our godly living
our neighbors may be won over to Christ.[4]

[1] Rom. 6:13; 12:1–2; 1 Pet. 2:5–10
[2] Matt. 5:16; 1 Cor. 6:19–20
[3] Matt. 7:17–18; Gal. 5:22–24; 2 Pet. 1:10–11
[4] Matt. 5:14–16; Rom. 14:17–19; 1 Pet. 2:12; 3:1–2

**87 Q. Can those be saved
who do not turn to God
from their ungrateful
and impenitent ways?**

A. By no means.
Scripture tells us that
no unchaste person,
no idolater, adulterer, thief,
no covetous person,
no drunkard, slanderer, robber,
or the like
is going to inherit the kingdom of God.[1]

[1] 1 Cor. 6:9–10; Gal. 5:19–21; Eph. 5:1–20; 1 John 3:14

LORD'S DAY 33

**88 Q. What is involved
in genuine repentance or conversion?**

A. Two things:
the dying-away of the old self,
and the coming-to-life of the new.[1]

[1] Rom. 6:1–11; 2 Cor. 5:17; Eph. 4:22–24; Col. 3:5–10

89 Q. What is the dying-away of the old self?

A. It is to be genuinely sorry for sin,
to hate it more and more,
and to run away from it.[1]

[1] Ps. 51:3–4, 17; Joel 2:12–13; Rom. 8:12–13; 2 Cor. 7:10

90 Q. What is the coming-to-life of the new self?

A. It is wholehearted joy in God through Christ[1]
and a delight to do every kind of good
as God wants us to.[2]

[1] Ps. 51:8, 12; Isa.57:15; Rom. 5:1; 14:17
[2] Rom. 6:10–11; Gal. 2:20

91 Q. What do we do that is good?

A. Only that which
arises out of true faith,[1]
conforms to God's law,[2]
and is done for his glory;[3]
and not that which is based
on what we think is right
or on established human tradition.[4]

[1] John 15:5; Heb. 11:6
[2] Lev. 18:4; 1 Sam. 15:22; Eph. 2:10
[3] 1 Cor. 10:31
[4] Deut. 12:32; Isa. 29:13; Ezek. 20:18–19; Matt. 15:7–9

LORD'S DAY 34

92 Q. What does the Lord say in his law?

  A. God spoke all these words:

The First Commandment
I am the LORD your God,
   who brought you out of Egypt,
   out of the land of slavery.
You shall have no other gods before me.

The Second Commandment
You shall not make for yourself an idol
   in the form of anything in heaven above
   or on the earth beneath
   or in the waters below.
You shall not bow down to them or worship them;
   for I, the LORD your God, am a jealous God,
   punishing the children for the sin of the fathers
      to the third and fourth generation
      of those who hate me,
   but showing love to a thousand generations of those
      who love me and keep my commandments.

The Third Commandment
You shall not misuse the name of the LORD your God,
   for the LORD will not hold anyone guiltless
   who misuses his name.

The Fourth Commandment
Remember the Sabbath day by keeping it holy.
Six days you shall labor and do all your work,
but the seventh day is a Sabbath to the LORD your God.
On it you shall not do any work,
   neither you, nor your son or daughter,
   nor your manservant or maidservant,
   nor your animals,
   nor the alien within your gates.
For in six days the LORD made
   the heavens and the earth, the sea,
   and all that is in them,
but he rested on the seventh day.
Therefore the LORD blessed the Sabbath day
and made it holy.

The Fifth Commandment
Honor your father and your mother,
   so that you may live long
   in the land the Lord your God is giving you.

The Sixth Commandment
You shall not murder.

The Seventh Commandment
You shall not commit adultery.

The Eighth Commandment
You shall not steal.

The Ninth Commandment
You shall not give false testimony
   against your neighbor.

The Tenth Commandment
You shall not covet your neighbor's house.
You shall not covet your neighbor's wife,
   or his manservant or maidservant,
   his ox or donkey,
   or anything that belongs to your neighbor.[1]

[1] Ex. 20:1–17; Deut. 5:6–21

93 Q. How are these commandments divided?

A. Into two tables.
The first has four commandments,
   teaching us what our relation to God should be.
The second has six commandments,
   teaching us what we owe our neighbor.[1]

[1] Matt. 22:37–39

**94 Q. What does the Lord require
in the first commandment?**

A. That I, not wanting to endanger my very salvation,
avoid and shun
all idolatry,[1] magic, superstitious rites,[2]
and prayer to saints or to other creatures.[3]

That I sincerely acknowledge the only true God,[4]
trust him alone,[5]
look to him for every good thing[6]
humbly[7] and patiently,[8]
love him,[9] fear him,[10] and honor him[11]
with all my heart.

In short,
that I give up anything
rather than go against his will in any way.[12]

[1] 1 Cor. 6:9–10; 10:5–14; 1 John 5:21
[2] Lev. 19:31; Deut. 18:9–12
[3] Matt. 4:10; Rev. 19:10; 22:8–9
[4] John 17:3
[5] Jer. 17:5, 7
[6] Ps. 104:27–28; James 1:17
[7] 1 Pet. 5:5–6
[8] Col. 1:11; Heb. 10:36
[9] Matt. 22:37 (Deut. 6:5)
[10] Prov. 9:10; 1 Pet. 1:17
[11] Matt. 4:10 (Deut. 6:13)
[12] Matt. 5:29–30; 10:37–39

95 Q. What is idolatry?

A. Idolatry is
having or inventing something in which one trusts
in place of or alongside of the only true God,
who has revealed himself in his Word.[1]

[1] 1 Chron. 16:26; Gal. 4:8–9; Eph. 5:5; Phil. 3:19

LORD'S DAY 35

**96 Q. What is God's will for us
in the second commandment?**

A. That we in no way make any image of God[1]
nor worship him in any other way
than he has commanded in his Word.[2]

[1] Deut. 4:15–19; Isa. 40:18–25; Acts 17:29; Rom. 1:22–23
[2] Lev. 10:1–7; 1 Sam. 15:22–23; John 4:23–24

**97 Q. May we then not make
any image at all?**

A. God can not and may not
be visibly portrayed in any way.

Although creatures may be portrayed,
yet God forbids making or having such images
if one's intention is to worship them
or to serve God through them.[1]

[1] Ex. 34:13–14, 17; 2 Kings 18:4–5

**98 Q. But may not images be permitted in the churches
as teaching aids for the unlearned?**

A. No, we shouldn't try to be wiser than God.
He wants his people instructed
by the living preaching of his Word—[1]
not by idols that cannot even talk.[2]

[1] Rom. 10:14–15, 17; 2 Tim. 3:16–17; 2 Pet. 1:19
[2] Jer. 10:8; Hab. 2:18–20

LORD'S DAY 36

**99 Q. What is God's will for us
in the third commandment?**

A. That we neither blaspheme nor misuse the name of God
by cursing,[1] perjury,[2] or unnecessary oaths,[3]
nor share in such horrible sins
by being silent bystanders.[4]

In a word, it requires
that we use the holy name of God
only with reverence and awe,[5]
so that we may properly
confess him,[6]
pray to him,[7]
and praise him in everything we do and say.[8]

[1] Lev. 24:10–17
[2] Lev. 19:12
[3] Matt. 5:37; James 5:12
[4] Lev. 5:1; Prov. 29:24
[5] Ps. 99:1–5; Jer. 4:2
[6] Matt. 10:32–33; Rom. 10:9–10
[7] Ps. 50:14–15; 1 Tim. 2:8
[8] Col. 3:17

**100 Q. Is blasphemy of God's name by swearing and cursing
really such serious sin
that God is angry also with those
who do not do all they can
to help prevent it and forbid it?**

A. Yes, indeed.[1]
No sin is greater,
no sin makes God more angry
than blaspheming his name.
That is why he commanded the death penalty for it.[2]

[1] Lev. 5:1
[2] Lev. 24:10–17

LORD'S DAY 37

101 Q. **But may we swear an oath in God's name**
       if we do it reverently?

   A. Yes, when the government demands it,
         or when necessity requires it,
            in order to maintain and promote truth and trustworthiness
            for God's glory and our neighbor's good.

   Such oaths are approved in God's Word[1]
   and were rightly used by Old and New Testament believers.[2]

   [1] Deut. 6:13; 10:20; Jer. 4:1–2; Heb. 6:16
   [2] Gen. 21:24; Josh. 9:15; 1 Kings 1:29–30; Rom. 1:9; 2 Cor. 1:23

102 Q. **May we swear by saints or other creatures?**

   A. No.
         A legitimate oath means calling upon God
         as the one who knows my heart
            to witness to my truthfulness
            and to punish me if I swear falsely.[1]
         No creature is worthy of such honor.[2]

   [1] Rom. 9:1; 2 Cor. 1:23
   [2] Matt. 5:34–37; 23:16–22; James 5:12

LORD'S DAY 38

**103 Q. What is God's will for you
in the fourth commandment?**

   A. First,
      that the gospel ministry and education for it be maintained,[1]
      and that, especially on the festive day of rest,
      I regularly attend the assembly of God's people[2]
         to learn what God's Word teaches,[3]
         to participate in the sacraments,[4]
         to pray to God publicly,[5]
         and to bring Christian offerings for the poor.[6]

     Second,
      that every day of my life
         I rest from my evil ways,
         let the Lord work in me through his Spirit,
         and so begin already in this life
      the eternal Sabbath.[7]

[1] Deut. 6:4–9, 20–25; 1 Cor. 9:13–14; 2 Tim. 2:2; 3:13–17; Tit. 1:5
[2] Deut. 12:5–12; Ps. 40:9–10; 68:26; Acts 2:42–47; Heb. 10:23–25
[3] Rom. 10:14–17; 1 Cor. 14:31–32; 1 Tim. 4:13
[4] 1 Cor. 11:23–25
[5] Col. 3:16; 1 Tim. 2:1
[6] Ps. 50:14; 1 Cor. 16:2; 2 Cor. 8 & 9
[7] Isa. 66:23; Heb. 4:9–11

LORD'S DAY 39

**104 Q. What is God's will for you
in the fifth commandment?**

   A. That I honor, love, and be loyal to
      my father and mother
      and all those in authority over me;
    that I obey and submit to them, as is proper,
      when they correct and punish me;[1]
    and also that I be patient with their failings—[2]
    for through them God chooses to rule us.[3]

[1] Ex. 21:17; Prov. 1:8; 4:1; Rom. 13:1–2; Eph. 5:21–22; 6:1–9; Col. 3:18–4:1
[2] Prov. 20:20; 23:22; 1 Pet. 2:18
[3] Matt. 22:21; Rom. 13:1–8; Eph. 6:1–9; Col. 3:18–21

LORD'S DAY 40

**105 Q. What is God's will for you
in the sixth commandment?**

A. I am not to belittle, insult, hate, or kill my neighbor—
not by my thoughts, my words, my look or gesture,
and certainly not by actual deeds—
and I am not to be party to this in others;[1]
rather, I am to put away all desire for revenge.[2]

I am not to harm or recklessly endanger myself either.[3]

Prevention of murder is also why
government is armed with the sword.[4]

[1] Gen. 9:6; Lev. 19:17–18; Matt. 5:21–22; 26:52
[2] Prov. 25:21–22; Matt. 18:35; Rom. 12:19; Eph. 4:26
[3] Matt. 4:7; 26:52; Rom. 13:11–14
[4] Gen. 9:6; Ex. 21:14; Rom. 13:4

106 Q. Does this commandment refer only to killing?

A. By forbidding murder God teaches us
that he hates the root of murder:
envy, hatred, anger, vindictiveness.[1]

In God's sight all such are murder.[2]

[1] Prov. 14:30; Rom. 1:29; 12:19; Gal. 5:19–21; 1 John 2:9–11
[2] 1 John 3:15

**107 Q. Is it enough then
that we do not kill our neighbor
in any such way?**

A. No.
By condemning envy, hatred, and anger
God tells us
to love our neighbors as ourselves,[1]
to be patient, peace-loving, gentle,
merciful, and friendly to them,[2]
to protect them from harm as much as we can,
and to do good even to our enemies.[3]

[1] Matt. 7:12; 22:39; Rom. 12:10
[2] Matt. 5:3–12; Luke 6:36; Rom. 12:10, 18; Gal. 6:1–2; Eph. 4:2; Col. 3:12; 1 Pet. 3:8
[3] Ex. 23:4–5; Matt. 5:44–45; Rom. 12:20–21 (Prov. 25:21–22)

LORD'S DAY 41

**108 Q. What is God's will for us
in the seventh commandment?**

A. God condemns all unchastity.[1]
We should therefore thoroughly detest it[2]
and, married or single,
live decent and chaste lives.[3]

[1] Lev. 18:30; Eph. 5:3–5
[2] Jude 22–23
[3] 1 Cor. 7:1–9; 1 Thess. 4:3–8; Heb. 13:4

**109 Q. Does God, in this commandment,
forbid only such scandalous sins as adultery?**

A. We are temples of the Holy Spirit, body and soul,
and God wants both to be kept clean and holy.
That is why he forbids
everything which incites unchastity,[1]
whether it be actions, looks, talk, thoughts, or desires.[2]

[1] 1 Cor. 15:33; Eph. 5:18
[2] Matt. 5:27–29; 1 Cor. 6:18–20; Eph. 5:3–4

LORD'S DAY 42

**110 Q. What does God forbid
in the eighth commandment?**

A. He forbids not only outright theft and robbery,
punishable by law.[1]

But in God's sight theft also includes
cheating and swindling our neighbor
by schemes made to appear legitimate,[2]
such as:
inaccurate measurements of weight, size, or volume;
fraudulent merchandising;
counterfeit money;
excessive interest;
or any other means forbidden by God.[3]

In addition he forbids all greed[4]
and pointless squandering of his gifts.[5]

[1] Ex. 22:1; 1 Cor. 5:9–10; 6:9–10
[2] Mic. 6:9–11; Luke 3:14; James 5:1–6
[3] Deut. 25:13–16; Ps. 15:5; Prov. 11:1; 12:22; Ezek. 45:9–12; Luke 6:35
[4] Luke 12:15; Eph. 5:5
[5] Prov. 21:20; 23:20–21; Luke 16:10–13

**111 Q. What does God require of you
in this commandment?**

A. That I do whatever I can
for my neighbor's good,
that I treat others
as I would like them to treat me,
and that I work faithfully
so that I may share with those in need.[1]

[1] Isa. 58:5–10; Matt. 7:12; Gal. 6:9–10; Eph. 4:28

LORD'S DAY 43

**112 Q. What is God's will for you
in the ninth commandment?**

    A. God's will is that I
        never give false testimony against anyone,
        twist no one's words,
        not gossip or slander,
        nor join in condemning anyone
           without a hearing or without a just cause.[1]

    Rather, in court and everywhere else,
    I should avoid lying and deceit of every kind;
        these are devices the devil himself uses,
        and they would call down on me God's intense anger.[2]
    I should love the truth,
        speak it candidly,
        and openly acknowledge it.[3]
    And I should do what I can
        to guard and advance my neighbor's good name.[4]

[1] Ps. 15; Prov. 19:5; Matt. 7:1; Luke 6:37; Rom. 1:28–32
[2] Lev. 19:11–12; Prov. 12:22; 13:5; John 8:44; Rev. 21:8
[3] 1 Cor. 13:6; Eph. 4:25
[4] 1 Pet. 3:8–9; 4:8

LORD'S DAY 44

**113 Q. What is God's will for you
in the tenth commandment?**

A. That not even the slightest thought or desire
contrary to any one of God's commandments
should ever arise in my heart.

Rather, with all my heart
I should always hate sin
and take pleasure in whatever is right.[1]

[1] Ps. 19:7–14; 139:23–24; Rom. 7:7–8

**114 Q. But can those converted to God
obey these commandments perfectly?**

A. No.
In this life even the holiest
have only a small beginning of this obedience.[1]

Nevertheless, with all seriousness of purpose,
they do begin to live
according to all, not only some,
of God's commandments.[2]

[1] Eccles. 7:20; Rom. 7:14–15; 1 Cor. 13:9; 1 John 1:8–10
[2] Ps. 1:1–2; Rom. 7:22–25; Phil. 3:12–16

**115 Q. No one in this life
can obey the Ten Commandments perfectly:
why then does God want them
preached so pointedly?**

A. First, so that the longer we live
the more we may come to know our sinfulness
and the more eagerly look to Christ
for forgiveness of sins and righteousness.[1]

Second, so that,
while praying to God for the grace of the Holy Spirit,
we may never stop striving
to be renewed more and more after God's image,
until after this life we reach our goal:
perfection.[2]

[1] Ps. 32:5; Rom. 3:19–26; 7:7, 24–25; 1 John 1:9
[2] 1 Cor. 9:24; Phil. 3:12–14; 1 John 3:1–3

Prayer

LORD'S DAY 45

116 Q. Why do Christians need to pray?

  A. Because prayer is the most important part
            of the thankfulness God requires of us.[1]
        And also because God gives his grace and Holy Spirit
        only to those who pray continually and groan inwardly,
            asking God for these gifts
            and thanking him for them.[2]

   [1] Ps. 50:14–15; 116:12–19; 1 Thess. 5:16–18
   [2] Matt. 7:7–8; Luke 11:9–13

**117 Q. How does God want us to pray
         so that he will listen to us?**

  A. First, we must pray from the heart
            to no other than the one true God,
                who has revealed himself in his Word,
            asking for everything he has commanded us to ask for.[1]

        Second, we must acknowledge our need and misery,
            hiding nothing,
            and humble ourselves in his majestic presence.[2]

        Third, we must rest on this unshakable foundation:
            even though we do not deserve it,
            God will surely listen to our prayer
                because of Christ our Lord.
            That is what he promised us in his Word.[3]

   [1] Ps. 145:18–20; John 4:22–24; Rom. 8:26–27; James 1:5; 1 John 5:14–15
   [2] 2 Chron. 7:14; Ps. 2:11; 34:18; 62:8; Isa. 66:2; Rev. 4
   [3] Dan. 9:17–19; Matt. 7:8; John 14:13–14; 16:23; Rom. 10:13; James 1:6

118 Q. What did God command us to pray for?

  A. Everything we need, spiritually and physically,[1]
        as embraced in the prayer
        Christ our Lord himself taught us.

   [1] James 1:17; Matt. 6:33

119 Q. What is this prayer?

    A. Our Father in heaven,
        hallowed be your name,
        your kingdom come,
        your will be done
           on earth as it is in heaven.
        Give us today our daily bread.
        Forgive us our debts,
           as we also have forgiven our debtors.
        And lead us not into temptation,
           but deliver us from the evil one.
        For yours is the kingdom
           and the power
           and the glory forever.
        Amen.[1]*

[1] Matt. 6:9–13; Luke 11:2–4

*Earlier and better manuscripts of Matthew 6 omit the words "For yours is . . . Amen."

LORD'S DAY 46

**120 Q. Why did Christ command us
to call God "our Father"?**

    A. At the very beginning of our prayer
Christ wants to kindle in us
what is basic to our prayer—
    the childlike awe and trust
    that God through Christ has become
our Father.

    Our fathers do not refuse us
    the things of this life;
God our Father will even less refuse to give us
    what we ask in faith.[1]

[1] Matt. 7:9–11; Luke 11:11–13

**121 Q. Why the words
"in heaven"?**

    A. These words teach us
    not to think of God's heavenly majesty
      as something earthly,[1]
    and to expect everything
      for body and soul
      from his almighty power.[2]

[1] Jer. 23:23–24; Acts 17:24–25
[2] Matt. 6:25–34; Rom. 8:31–32

LORD'S DAY 47

122 Q. What does the first request mean?

A. *Hallowed be your name* means,

Help us to really know you,[1]
to bless, worship, and praise you
   for all your works
   and for all that shines forth from them:
      your almighty power, wisdom, kindness,
      justice, mercy, and truth.[2]

And it means,

Help us to direct all our living—
   what we think, say, and do—
so that your name will never be blasphemed because of us
but always honored and praised.[3]

[1] Jer. 9:23–24; 31:33–34; Matt. 16:17; John 17:3
[2] Ex. 34:5–8; Ps. 145; Jer. 32:16–20; Luke 1:46–55, 68–75; Rom. 11:33–36
[3] Ps. 115:1; Matt. 5:16

LORD'S DAY 48

123 Q. What does the second request mean?

A. *Your kingdom come* means,

Rule us by your Word and Spirit in such a way
    that more and more we submit to you.[1]

Keep your church strong, and add to it.[2]

Destroy the devil's work;
destroy every force which revolts against you
and every conspiracy against your Word.[3]

Do this until your kingdom is so complete and perfect
    that in it you are
        all in all.[4]

[1] Ps. 119:5, 105; 143:10; Matt. 6:33
[2] Ps. 122:6–9; Matt. 16:18; Acts 2:42–47
[3] Rom. 16:20; 1 John 3:8
[4] Rom. 8:22–23; 1 Cor. 15:28; Rev. 22:17, 20

LORD'S DAY 49

124 Q. What does the third request mean?

A. *Your will be done on earth as it is in heaven* means,

Help us and all people
to reject our own wills
and to obey your will without any back talk.
Your will alone is good.[1]

Help us one and all to carry out the work we are called to,[2]
as willingly and faithfully as the angels in heaven.[3]

[1] Matt. 7:21; 16:24–26; Luke 22:42; Rom. 12:1–2; Tit. 2:11–12
[2] 1 Cor. 7:17–24; Eph. 6:5–9
[3] Ps. 103:20–21

LORD'S DAY 50

125 Q. What does the fourth request mean?

    A. *Give us today our daily bread* means,

Do take care of all our physical needs[1]
so that we come to know
    that you are the only source of everything good,[2]
    and that neither our work and worry
    nor your gifts
    can do us any good without your blessing.[3]

And so help us to give up our trust in creatures
and to put trust in you alone.[4]

[1] Ps. 104:27–30; 145:15–16; Matt. 6:25–34
[2] Acts 14:17; 17:25; James 1:17
[3] Deut. 8:3; Ps. 37:16; 127:1–2; 1 Cor. 15:58
[4] Ps. 55:22; 62; 146; Jer. 17:5–8; Heb. 13:5–6

LORD'S DAY 51

126 Q. What does the fifth request mean?

A. *Forgive us our debts,*
as we also have forgiven our debtors means,

Because of Christ's blood,
do not hold against us, poor sinners that we are,
   any of the sins we do
   or the evil that constantly clings to us.[1]

Forgive us just as we are fully determined,
   as evidence of your grace in us,
to forgive our neighbors.[2]

[1] Ps. 51:1–7; 143:2; Rom. 8:1; 1 John 2:1–2
[2] Matt. 6:14–15; 18:21–35

LORD'S DAY 52

127 Q. What does the sixth request mean?

A. *And lead us not into temptation,*
but deliver us from the evil one means,

By ourselves we are too weak
to hold our own even for a moment.[1]

And our sworn enemies—
the devil,[2] the world,[3] and our own flesh—[4]
never stop attacking us.

And so, Lord,
uphold us and make us strong
with the strength of your Holy Spirit,
so that we may not go down to defeat
in this spiritual struggle,[5]
but may firmly resist our enemies
until we finally win the complete victory.[6]

[1] Ps. 103:14–16; John 15:1–5
[2] 2 Cor. 11:14; Eph. 6:10–13; 1 Pet. 5:8
[3] John 15:18–21
[4] Rom. 7:23; Gal. 5:17
[5] Matt. 10:19–20; 26:41; Mark 13:33; Rom. 5:3–5
[6] 1 Cor. 10:13; 1 Thess. 3:13; 5:23

128 Q. What does your conclusion to this prayer mean?

A. *For yours is the kingdom*
and the power
and the glory forever means,

We have made all these requests of you
because, as our all-powerful king,
you not only want to,
but are able to give us all that is good;[1]
and because your holy name,
and not we ourselves,
should receive all the praise, forever.[2]

[1] Rom. 10:11–13; 2 Pet. 2:9
[2] Ps. 115:1; John 14:13

129 Q. What does that little word "Amen" express?

A. *Amen* means,

This is sure to be!

It is even more sure
that God listens to my prayer,
than that I really desire
what I pray for.[1]

[1] Isa. 65:24; 2 Cor. 1:20; 2 Tim. 2:13

The Belgic Confession

Article 1: *The Only God*

We all believe in our hearts
and confess with our mouths
that there is a single
and simple
spiritual being,
whom we call God—

> eternal,
> incomprehensible,
> invisible,
> unchangeable,
> infinite,
> almighty;

> completely wise,
> just,
> and good,
> and the overflowing source
>   of all good.

The oldest of the doctrinal standards of the Christian Reformed Church is the *Confession of Faith*, popularly known as the *Belgic Confession*, following the seventeenth-century Latin designation "Confessio Belgica." "Belgica" referred to the whole of the Netherlands, both north and south, which today is divided into the Netherlands and Belgium. The confession's chief author was Guido de Brès, a preacher of the Reformed churches of the Netherlands, who died a martyr to the faith in the year 1567. During the sixteenth century the churches in this country were exposed to the most terrible persecution by the Roman Catholic government. To protest against this cruel oppression, and to prove to the persecutors that the adherents of the Reformed faith were not rebels, as was laid to their charge, but law-abiding citizens who professed the true Christian doctrine according to the Holy Scriptures, de Brès prepared this confession in the year 1561. In the following year a copy was sent to King Philip II, together with an address in which the petitioners declared that they were ready to obey the government in all lawful things, but that they would "offer their backs to stripes, their tongues to knives, their mouths to gags, and their whole bodies to the fire," rather than deny the truth expressed in this confession.

Although the immediate purpose of securing freedom from persecution was not attained, and de Brès himself fell as one of the many thousands who sealed their faith with their lives, his work has endured and will continue to endure. In its composition the author availed himself to some extent of a confession of the Reformed churches in France, written chiefly by John Calvin, published two years earlier. The work of de Brès, however, is not a mere revision of Calvin's work, but an independent composition. In 1566 the text of this confession was revised at a synod held at Antwerp. In the Netherlands it was at once gladly received by the churches, and it was adopted by national synods held during the last three decades of the sixteenth century. The text, not the contents, was revised again at the Synod of Dort in 1618–19 and adopted as one of the doctrinal standards to which all officebearers in the Reformed churches were required to subscribe. The confession stands as one of the best symbolical statements of Reformed doctrine. The translation presented here is based on the French text of 1619 and was adopted by the Synod of 1985 of the Christian Reformed Church.

Article 2: *The Means by Which We Know God*

We know him by two means:

First, by the creation, preservation, and government
of the universe,
since that universe is before our eyes
like a beautiful book
   in which all creatures,
   great and small,
   are as letters
   to make us ponder
   the invisible things of God:
      his eternal power
      and his divinity,
      as the apostle Paul says in Romans 1:20.

   All these things are enough to convict men
   and to leave them without excuse.

Second, he makes himself known to us more openly
by his holy and divine Word,
as much as we need in this life,
   for his glory
   and for the salvation of his own.

Article 3: *The Written Word of God*

We confess that this Word of God
was not sent nor delivered by the will of men,
but that holy men of God spoke,
being moved by the Holy Spirit,
   as Peter says.[1]

Afterwards our God—
   because of the special care he has
   for us and our salvation—
commanded his servants,
the prophets and apostles,
to commit this revealed Word to writing.
He himself wrote
with his own finger
the two tables of the law.

Therefore we call such writings
holy and divine Scriptures.

[1] 2 Pet. 1:21

Article 4: *The Canonical Books*

We include in the Holy Scripture the two volumes
of the Old and New Testaments.
They are canonical books
with which there can be no quarrel at all.

In the church of God the list is as follows:
In the Old Testament,
   the five books of Moses—
      Genesis, Exodus, Leviticus, Numbers, Deuteronomy;
   the books of Joshua, Judges, and Ruth;
   the two books of Samuel, and two of Kings;
   the two books of Chronicles, called Paralipomenon;
   the first book of Ezra; Nehemiah, Esther, Job;
   the Psalms of David;
   the three books of Solomon—
      Proverbs, Ecclesiastes, and the Song;
   the four major prophets—
      Isaiah, Jeremiah, Ezekiel, Daniel;
   and then the other twelve minor prophets—
      Hosea, Joel, Amos, Obadiah,
      Jonah, Micah, Nahum, Habakkuk,
      Zephaniah, Haggai, Zechariah, Malachi.

In the New Testament,
   the four gospels—
      Matthew, Mark, Luke, and John;
   the Acts of the Apostles;
   the fourteen letters of Paul—
      to the Romans;
      the two letters to the Corinthians;
      to the Galatians, Ephesians, Philippians, and Colossians;
      the two letters to the Thessalonians;
      the two letters to Timothy;
      to Titus, Philemon, and to the Hebrews;
   the seven letters of the other apostles—
      one of James;
      two of Peter;
      three of John;
      one of Jude;
   and the Revelation of the apostle John.

Article 5: *The Authority of Scripture*

We receive all these books
and these only
as holy and canonical,
for the regulating, founding, and establishing
of our faith.

And we believe
without a doubt
all things contained in them—
   not so much because the church
   receives and approves them as such
   but above all because the Holy Spirit
   testifies in our hearts
   that they are from God,
   and also because they
   prove themselves
   to be from God.

   For even the blind themselves are able to see
   that the things predicted in them
   do happen.

Article 6: *The Difference Between Canonical*
and Apocryphal Books

We distinguish between these holy books
and the apocryphal ones,
   which are the third and fourth books of Esdras;
   the books of Tobit, Judith, Wisdom, Jesus Sirach, Baruch;
   what was added to the Story of Esther;
   the Song of the Three Children in the Furnace;
   the Story of Susanna;
   the Story of Bel and the Dragon;
   the Prayer of Manasseh;
   and the two books of Maccabees.

The church may certainly read these books
and learn from them
as far as they agree with the canonical books.
But they do not have such power and virtue
that one could confirm
from their testimony
any point of faith or of the Christian religion.
Much less can they detract
from the authority
of the other holy books.

Article 7: *The Sufficiency of Scripture*

We believe
that this Holy Scripture contains
the will of God completely
and that everything one must believe
to be saved
is sufficiently taught in it.

For since the entire manner of service
which God requires of us
is described in it at great length,
no one—
   even an apostle
   or an angel from heaven,
   as Paul says—[2]
ought to teach other than
what the Holy Scriptures have
already taught us.

For since it is forbidden
to add to or subtract from the Word of God,[3]
this plainly demonstrates
that the teaching is perfect
and complete in all respects.

Therefore we must not consider human writings—
   no matter how holy their authors may have been—
equal to the divine writings;
nor may we put custom,
nor the majority,
nor age,
nor the passage of time or persons,
nor councils, decrees, or official decisions
above the truth of God,
   for truth is above everything else.

For all human beings are liars by nature
and more vain than vanity itself.

Therefore we reject with all our hearts
everything that does not agree
with this infallible rule,
   as we are taught to do by the apostles
   when they say,
      "Test the spirits
      to see if they are of God,"[4]
   and also,

"If anyone comes to you
and does not bring this teaching,
do not receive him
into your house."[5]

2 Gal. 1:8
3 Deut. 12:32; Rev. 22:18–19
4 1 John 4:1
5 2 John 10

Article 8: *The Trinity*

In keeping with this truth and Word of God
we believe in one God,
who is one single essence,
in whom there are three persons,
really, truly, and eternally distinct
according to their incommunicable properties—
   namely,
      Father,
      Son,
      and Holy Spirit.
The Father
   is the cause,
   origin,
   and source of all things,
      visible as well as invisible.

The Son
   is the Word,
   the Wisdom,
   and the image
      of the Father.

The Holy Spirit
   is the eternal power
   and might,
      proceeding from the Father and the Son.

Nevertheless,
this distinction does not divide God into three,
   since Scripture teaches us
   that the Father, the Son, and the Holy Spirit
   each has his own subsistence
   distinguished by characteristics—
   yet in such a way
   that these three persons are
   only one God.

It is evident then
that the Father is not the Son
and that the Son is not the Father,
and that likewise the Holy Spirit is
neither the Father nor the Son.

Nevertheless,
these persons,
thus distinct,
are neither divided
nor fused or mixed together.

> For the Father did not take on flesh,
> nor did the Spirit,
> but only the Son.

> The Father was never
> without his Son,
> nor without his Holy Spirit,
> since all these are equal from eternity,
> in one and the same essence.

There is neither a first nor a last,
for all three are one
in truth and power,
in goodness and mercy.

Article 9: *The Scriptural Witness on the Trinity*

All these things we know
from the testimonies of Holy Scripture
as well as from the effects of the persons,
especially from those we feel within ourselves.

The testimonies of the Holy Scriptures,
which teach us to believe in this Holy Trinity,
are written in many places of the Old Testament,
which need not be enumerated
but only chosen with discretion.

> In the book of Genesis God says,
>> "Let us make man in our image,
>> according to our likeness."
> So "God created man in his own image"—
>> indeed, "male and female he created them."[6]
>> "Behold, man has become like one of us."[7]

It appears from this
that there is a plurality of persons
within the Deity,
    when he says,
    "Let us make man in our image"—
and afterwards he indicates the unity
    when he says,
    "God created."

It is true that he does not say here
how many persons there are—
but what is somewhat obscure to us
in the Old Testament
is very clear in the New.

For when our Lord was baptized in the Jordan,
the voice of the Father was heard saying,
    "This is my dear Son";[8]
the Son was seen in the water;
and the Holy Spirit appeared in the form of a dove.

So, in the baptism of all believers
this form was prescribed by Christ:
    "Baptize all people in the name
    of the Father,
    and of the Son,
    and of the Holy Spirit."[9]

In the Gospel according to Luke
the angel Gabriel says to Mary,
the mother of our Lord:
    "The Holy Spirit will come upon you,
    and the power of the Most High will overshadow you;
    and therefore that holy one to be born of you
    shall be called the Son of God."[10]

And in another place it says:
    "The grace of our Lord Jesus Christ,
    and the love of God,
    and the fellowship of the Holy Spirit
    be with you."[11]

    "There are three who bear witness in heaven—
    the Father, the Word, and the Holy Spirit—
    and these three are one."[12]

In all these passages we are fully taught
that there are three persons
in the one and only divine essence.
And although this doctrine surpasses human understanding,
we nevertheless believe it now,
    through the Word,
waiting to know and enjoy it fully
    in heaven.

Furthermore,
we must note the particular works and activities
of these three persons in relation to us.
    The Father is called our Creator,
        by reason of his power.
    The Son is our Savior and Redeemer,
        by his blood.
    The Holy Spirit is our Sanctifier,
        by his living in our hearts.

This doctrine of the Holy Trinity
has always been maintained in the true church,
    from the time of the apostles until the present,
    against Jews, Muslims,
    and certain false Christians and heretics,
        such as Marcion, Mani,
        Praxeas, Sabellius, Paul of Samosata, Arius,
        and others like them,
        who were rightly condemned by the holy fathers.

And so,
in this matter we willingly accept
the three ecumenical creeds—
the Apostles', Nicene, and Athanasian—
as well as what the ancient fathers decided
in agreement with them.

[6] Gen. 1:26–27
[7] Gen. 3:22
[8] Matt. 3:17
[9] Matt. 28:19
[10] Luke 1:35
[11] 2 Cor. 13:14
[12] 1 John 5:7 (KJV)

Article 10: *The Deity of Christ*

We believe that Jesus Christ,
according to his divine nature,
is the only Son of God—
    eternally begotten,
    not made nor created,
        for then he would be a creature.

He is one in essence with the Father;
coeternal;
the exact image of the person of the Father
and the "reflection of his glory,"[13]
    being in all things like him.

He is the Son of God
not only from the time he assumed our nature
but from all eternity,
    as the following testimonies teach us
    when they are taken together.

    Moses says that God "created the world";[14]
    and John says that "all things were created by the Word,"[15]
        which he calls God.
    The apostle says that "God made the world by his Son."[16]
    He also says that "God created all things by Jesus Christ."[17]

And so it must follow
that he who is called God, the Word, the Son, and Jesus Christ
already existed when all things were created by him.
Therefore the prophet Micah says
that his origin is "from ancient times,
    from eternity."[18]
And the apostle says
that he has "neither beginning of days
    nor end of life."[19]

So then,
he is the true eternal God,
the Almighty,
whom we invoke,
worship,
and serve.

[13] Col. 1:15; Heb. 1:3
[14] Gen. 1:1
[15] John 1:3
[16] Heb. 1:2
[17] Col. 1:16
[18] Mic. 5:2
[19] Heb. 7:3

Article 11: *The Deity of the Holy Spirit*

We believe and confess also
that the Holy Spirit proceeds eternally
from the Father and the Son—
    neither made,
    nor created,
    nor begotten,
    but only proceeding
    from the two of them.

In regard to order,
he is the third person of the Trinity—
    of one and the same essence,
    and majesty,
    and glory,
    with the Father and the Son.

He is true and eternal God,
    as the Holy Scriptures teach us.

Article 12: *The Creation of All Things*

We believe that the Father
created heaven and earth and all other creatures
from nothing,
when it seemed good to him,
by his Word—
    that is to say,
    by his Son.

He has given all creatures
their being, form, and appearance,
and their various functions
    for serving their Creator.

Even now
he also sustains and governs them all,
according to his eternal providence,
and by his infinite power,
    that they may serve man,
    in order that man may serve God.

He has also created the angels good,
that they might be his messengers
and serve his elect.

Some of them have fallen
   from the excellence in which God created them
   into eternal perdition;
and the others have persisted and remained
   in their orginal state,
   by the grace of God.

The devils and evil spirits are so corrupt
that they are enemies of God
and of everything good.
They lie in wait for the church
and every member of it
like thieves,
   with all their power,
to destroy and spoil everything
   by their deceptions.

So then,
by their own wickedness
they are condemned to everlasting damnation,
   daily awaiting their torments.

For that reason
we detest the error of the Sadducees,
   who deny that there are spirits and angels,
and also the error of the Manicheans,
   who say that the devils originated by themselves,
   being evil by nature,
      without having been corrupted.

Article 13: *The Doctrine of God's Providence*

We believe that this good God,
   after he created all things,
did not abandon them to chance or fortune
but leads and governs them
   according to his holy will,
in such a way that nothing happens in this world
without his orderly arrangement.

Yet God is not the author of,
nor can he be charged with,
the sin that occurs.
For his power and goodness
are so great and incomprehensible
that he arranges and does his work very well and justly
even when the devils and wicked men act unjustly.

We do not wish to inquire
    with undue curiosity
into what he does that surpasses human understanding
    and is beyond our ability to comprehend.
But in all humility and reverence
we adore the just judgments of God,
which are hidden from us,
    being content to be Christ's disciples,
        so as to learn only what he shows us in his Word,
            without going beyond those limits.

This doctrine gives us unspeakable comfort
since it teaches us
that nothing can happen to us by chance
but only by the arrangement of our gracious
heavenly Father.
He watches over us with fatherly care,
keeping all creatures under his control,
so that not one of the hairs on our heads
(for they are all numbered)
nor even a little bird
can fall to the ground
without the will of our Father.[20]

In this thought we rest,
knowing that he holds in check
the devils and all our enemies,
    who cannot hurt us
    without his permission and will.

For that reason we reject
the damnable error of the Epicureans,
    who say that God involves himself in nothing
    and leaves everything to chance.

[20] Matt. 10:29–30

Article 14: *The Creation and Fall of Man*

We believe
that God created man from the dust of the earth
and made and formed him in his image and likeness—
    good, just, and holy;
    able by his own will to conform
    in all things
    to the will of God.

But when he was in honor
he did not understand it[21]
and did not recognize his excellence.
But he subjected himself willingly to sin
and consequently to death and the curse,
    lending his ear to the word of the devil.

For he transgressed the commandment of life,
    which he had received,
and by his sin he separated himself from God,
    who was his true life,
having corrupted his entire nature.

So he made himself guilty
and subject to physical and spiritual death,
    having become wicked,
    perverse,
    and corrupt in all his ways.
He lost all his excellent gifts
    which he had received from God,
and he retained none of them
except for small traces
    which are enough to make him
    inexcusable.

Moreover, all the light in us is turned to darkness,
as the Scripture teaches us:
    "The light shone in the darkness,
    and the darkness did not receive it."[22]
Here John calls men "darkness."

Therefore we reject everything taught to the contrary
concerning man's free will,
since man is nothing but the slave of sin
and cannot do a thing
unless it is "given him from heaven."[23]

For who can boast of being able
to do anything good by himself,
since Christ says,
    "No one can come to me
    unless my Father who sent me
    draws him"?[24]

Who can glory in his own will
    when he understands that "the mind of the flesh
    is enmity against God"?[25]
Who can speak of his own knowledge
    in view of the fact that "the natural man
    does not understand the things of the Spirit of God"?[26]

In short,
who can produce a single thought,
    since he knows that we are "not able to think a thing"
    about ourselves,
    by ourselves,
    but that "our ability is from God"?[27]

And therefore,
what the apostle says
ought rightly to stand fixed and firm:
    "God works within us both to will and to do
    according to his good pleasure."[28]

For there is no understanding nor will
conforming to God's understanding and will
apart from Christ's involvement,
    as he teaches us when he says,
    "Without me you can do nothing."[29]

[21] Ps. 49:20
[22] John 1:5
[23] John 3:27
[24] John 6:44
[25] Rom. 8:7
[26] 1 Cor. 2:14
[27] 2 Cor. 3:5
[28] Phil. 2:13
[29] John 15:5

Article 15: *The Doctrine of Original Sin*

We believe
that by the disobedience of Adam
original sin has been spread
through the whole human race.

It is a corruption of all nature—
an inherited depravity which even infects small infants
   in their mother's womb,
and the root which produces in man
   every sort of sin.
It is therefore so vile and enormous in God's sight
that it is enough to condemn the human race,
and it is not abolished
   or wholly uprooted
   even by baptism,
      seeing that sin constantly boils forth
      as though from a contaminated spring.

Nevertheless,
it is not imputed to God's children
for their condemnation
but is forgiven
by his grace and mercy—
   not to put them to sleep
   but so that the awareness of this corruption
   might often make believers groan
   as they long to be set free
   from the "body of this death."[30]

Therefore we reject the error of the Pelagians
who say that this sin is nothing else than a matter of
imitation.

[30] Rom. 7:24

Article 16: *The Doctrine of Election*

We believe that—
   all Adam's descendants having thus fallen
   into perdition and ruin
   by the sin of the first man—
God showed himself to be as he is:
merciful and just.

He is merciful
in withdrawing and saving from this perdition those whom he,
   in his eternal and unchangeable counsel,
has elected and chosen in Jesus Christ our Lord
   by his pure goodness,
   without any consideration of their works.

He is just
in leaving the others in their ruin and fall
   into which they plunged themselves.

Article 17: *The Recovery of Fallen Man*

We believe that our good God,
by his marvelous wisdom and goodness,
   seeing that man had plunged himself in this manner
   into both physical and spiritual death
   and made himself completely miserable,
set out to find him,
though man,
   trembling all over,
was fleeing from him.

And he comforted him,
promising to give him his Son,
   "born of a woman,"[31]
to crush the head of the serpent,[32]
and to make him blessed.

[31] Gal. 4:4
[32] Gen. 3:15

Article 18: *The Incarnation*

So then we confess
that God fulfilled the promise
   which he had made to the early fathers
   by the mouth of his holy prophets
when he sent his only and eternal Son
into the world
at the time set by him.

The Son took the "form of a servant"
and was made in the "likeness of man,"[33]
    truly assuming a real human nature,
    with all its weaknesses,
    except for sin;
    being conceived in the womb of the blessed virgin Mary
    by the power of the Holy Spirit,
    without male participation.

And he not only assumed human nature
    as far as the body is concerned
but also a real human soul,
    in order that he might be a real human being.
For since the soul had been lost as well as the body
he had to assume them both
to save them both together.

Therefore we confess,
    against the heresy of the Anabaptists
    who deny that Christ assumed human flesh
        from his mother,
that he "shared the very flesh and blood of children";[34]
that he is "fruit of the loins of David" according to the flesh;[35]
"born of the seed of David" according to the flesh;[36]
"fruit of the womb of the virgin Mary";[37]
"born of a woman";[38]
"the seed of David";[39]
"a shoot from the root of Jesse";[40]
"the offspring of Judah,"[41]
    having descended from the Jews according to the flesh;
"from the seed of Abraham"—
    for he "assumed Abraham's seed"
    and was "made like his brothers
        except for sin."[42]

In this way he is truly our Immanuel—
    that is: "God with us."[43]

[33] Phil. 2:7
[34] Heb. 2:14
[35] Acts 2:30
[36] Rom. 1:3
[37] Luke 1:42
[38] Gal. 4:4
[39] 2 Tim. 2:8
[40] Rom. 15:12
[41] Heb. 7:14
[42] Heb. 2:17; 4:15
[43] Matt. 1:23

Article 19: *The Two Natures of Christ*

We believe that by being thus conceived
the person of the Son has been inseparably united
and joined together
with human nature,
   in such a way that there are not two Sons of God,
   nor two persons,
   but two natures united in a single person,
   with each nature retaining its own distinct properties.

Thus his divine nature has always remained uncreated,
   without beginning of days or end of life,[44]
   filling heaven and earth.

His human nature has not lost its properties
but continues to have those of a creature—
   it has a beginning of days;
   it is of a finite nature
   and retains all that belongs to a real body.
   And even though he,
   by his resurrection,
   gave it immortality,
   that nonetheless did not change
   the reality of his human nature;
   for our salvation and resurrection
   depend also on the reality of his body.

But these two natures
are so united together in one person
that they are not even separated by his death.

So then,
what he committed to his Father when he died
was a real human spirit which left his body.
But meanwhile his divine nature remained
united with his human nature
   even when he was lying in the grave;
and his deity never ceased to be in him,
   just as it was in him when he was a little child,
   though for a while it did not show itself as such.

These are the reasons why we confess him
to be true God and true man—
   true God in order to conquer death
     by his power,
   and true man that he might die for us
     in the weakness of his flesh.

[44] Heb. 7:3

Article 20: *The Justice and Mercy of God in Christ*

We believe that God—
  who is perfectly merciful
  and also very just—
sent his Son to assume the nature
in which the disobedience had been committed,
  in order to bear in it the punishment of sin
  by his most bitter passion and death.

So God made known his justice toward his Son,
  who was charged with our sin,
and he poured out his goodness and mercy on us,
  who are guilty and worthy of damnation,
giving to us his Son to die,
  by a most perfect love,
and raising him to life
  for our justification,
    in order that by him
    we might have immortality
    and eternal life.

Article 21: *The Atonement*

We believe
that Jesus Christ is a high priest forever
according to the order of Melchizedek—
  made such by an oath—
and that he presented himself
in our name
before his Father,
to appease his wrath
with full satisfaction
  by offering himself
    on the tree of the cross
  and pouring out his precious blood
    for the cleansing of our sins,
    as the prophets had predicted.

For it is written
that "the chastisement of our peace"
was placed on the Son of God
and that "we are healed by his wounds."
He was "led to death as a lamb";
he was "numbered among sinners"[45]
and condemned as a criminal by Pontius Pilate,
  though Pilate had declared
  that he was innocent.

So he paid back
what he had not stolen,[46]
and he suffered—
the "just for the unjust,"[47]
in both his body and his soul—
in such a way that
when he sensed the horrible punishment
required by our sins
his sweat became like "big drops of blood
falling on the ground."[48]
He cried, "My God, my God,
why have you abandoned me?"[49]

And he endured all this
for the forgiveness of our sins.

Therefore we rightly say with Paul that
we "know nothing but Jesus and him crucified";[50]
we consider all things as "dung
for the excellence of the knowledge
of our Lord Jesus Christ."[51]
We find all comforts in his wounds
and have no need to seek or invent any other means
to reconcile ourselves with God
than this one and only sacrifice,
once made,
which renders believers perfect
forever.

This is also why
the angel of God called him Jesus—
that is, "Savior"—
because he would save his people
from their sins.[52]

[45] Isa. 53:4–12
[46] Ps. 69:4
[47] 1 Pet. 3:18
[48] Luke 22:44
[49] Matt. 27:46
[50] 1 Cor. 2:2
[51] Phil. 3:8
[52] Matt. 1:21

Article 22: *The Righteousness of Faith*

We believe that
for us to acquire the true knowledge of this great mystery
the Holy Spirit kindles in our hearts a true faith
that embraces Jesus Christ,
    with all his merits,
and makes him its own,
and no longer looks for anything
    apart from him.

For it must necessarily follow
that either all that is required for our salvation
is not in Christ or,
if all is in him,
then he who has Christ by faith
has his salvation entirely.

Therefore,
to say that Christ is not enough
but that something else is needed as well
is a most enormous blasphemy against God—
    for it then would follow
    that Jesus Christ is only half a Savior.
And therefore we justly say with Paul
that we are justified "by faith alone"
or by faith "apart from works."[53]

However,
we do not mean,
properly speaking,
that it is faith itself that justifies us—
    for faith is only the instrument
    by which we embrace Christ,
    our righteousness.

But Jesus Christ is our righteousness
    in making available to us all his merits
    and all the holy works he has done
    for us and in our place.
And faith is the instrument
    that keeps us in communion with him
    and with all his benefits.

When those benefits are made ours
they are more than enough to absolve us
of our sins.

[53] Rom. 3:28

Article 23: *The Justification of Sinners*

We believe
that our blessedness lies in the forgiveness of our sins
because of Jesus Christ,
and that in it our righteousness before God is contained,
    as David and Paul teach us
    when they declare that man blessed
    to whom God grants righteousness
    apart from works.[54]

And the same apostle says
that we are justified "freely" or "by grace"
through redemption in Jesus Christ.[55]
And therefore we cling to this foundation,
which is firm forever,
    giving all glory to God,
    humbling ourselves,
    and recognizing ourselves as we are;
    not claiming a thing for ourselves or our merits
    and leaning and resting
        on the sole obedience of Christ crucified,
            which is ours when we believe in him.

That is enough to cover all our sins
and to make us confident,
freeing the conscience from the fear, dread, and terror
    of God's approach,
without doing what our first father, Adam, did,
    who trembled as he tried to cover himself
        with fig leaves.

In fact,
if we had to appear before God relying—
    no matter how little—
on ourselves or some other creature,
then, alas, we would be swallowed up.

Therefore everyone must say with David:
"Lord, do not enter into judgment with your servants,
    for before you no living person shall be justified."[56]

[54] Ps. 32:1; Rom. 4:6
[55] Rom. 3:24
[56] Ps. 143:2

Article 24: *The Sanctification of Sinners*

We believe that this true faith,
    produced in man by the hearing of God's Word
    and by the work of the Holy Spirit,
regenerates him and makes him a "new man,"[57]
    causing him to live the "new life"[58]
    and freeing him from the slavery of sin.

Therefore,
far from making people cold
toward living in a pious and holy way,
this justifying faith,
quite to the contrary,
so works within them that
    apart from it
they will never do a thing out of love for God
but only out of love for themselves
and fear of being condemned.

So then, it is impossible
for this holy faith to be unfruitful in a human being,
seeing that we do not speak of an empty faith
but of what Scripture calls
"faith working through love,"[59]
    which leads a man to do by himself
    the works that God has commanded
        in his Word.

These works,
    proceeding from the good root of faith,
are good and acceptable to God,
    since they are all sanctified by his grace.
Yet they do not count toward our justification—
    for by faith in Christ we are justified,
    even before we do good works.
        Otherwise they could not be good,
        any more than the fruit of a tree could be good
        if the tree is not good in the first place.

So then, we do good works,
but not for merit—
    for what would we merit?
Rather, we are indebted to God for the good works we do,
    and not he to us,
since it is he who "works in us both to will and do
    according to his good pleasure"[60]—
thus keeping in mind what is written:
    "When you have done all that is commanded you,
    then you shall say, 'We are unworthy servants;
    we have done what it was our duty to do.' "[61]

Yet we do not wish to deny
that God rewards good works—
but it is by his grace
that he crowns his gifts.

Moreover,
although we do good works
we do not base our salvation on them;
    for we cannot do any work
    that is not defiled by our flesh
    and also worthy of punishment.
And even if we could point to one,
    memory of a single sin is enough
    for God to reject that work.

So we would always be in doubt,
    tossed back and forth
    without any certainty,
and our poor consciences would be tormented constantly
    if they did not rest on the merit
    of the suffering and death of our Savior.

[57] 2 Cor. 5:17
[58] Rom. 6:4
[59] Gal. 5:6
[60] Phil. 2:13
[61] Luke 17:10

Article 25: *The Fulfillment of the Law*

We believe
that the ceremonies and symbols of the law have ended
    with the coming of Christ,
and that all foreshadowings have come to an end,
so that the use of them ought to be abolished
    among Christians.
Yet the truth and substance of these things
remain for us in Jesus Christ,
    in whom they have been fulfilled.

Nevertheless,
we continue to use the witnesses
drawn from the law and prophets
    to confirm us in the gospel
    and to regulate our lives with full integrity
        for the glory of God,
        according to his will.

Article 26: *The Intercession of Christ*

We believe that we have no access to God
except through the one and only Mediator and Intercessor:
Jesus Christ the Righteous.[62]

He therefore was made man,
uniting together the divine and human natures,
so that we human beings might have access to the divine Majesty.
Otherwise we would have no access.

But this Mediator,
    whom the Father has appointed between himself and us,
ought not terrify us by his greatness,
    so that we have to look for another one,
        according to our fancy.
For neither in heaven nor among the creatures on earth
is there anyone who loves us
more than Jesus Christ does.
    Although he was "in the form of God,"
    he nevertheless "emptied himself,"
    taking the form of "a man" and "a servant" for us;[63]
    and he made himself "completely like his brothers."[64]

Suppose we had to find another intercessor.
  Who would love us more than he who gave his life for us,
    even though "we were his enemies"?[65]
And suppose we had to find one who has prestige and power.
  Who has as much of these as he who is seated
    "at the right hand of the Father,"[66]
  and who has all power
    "in heaven and on earth"?[67]
  And who will be heard more readily
    than God's own dearly beloved Son?

So then, sheer unbelief has led to the practice
of dishonoring the saints,
instead of honoring them.
That was something the saints never did nor asked for,
but which in keeping with their duty,
  as appears from their writings,
they consistently refused.

We should not plead here
that we are unworthy—
  for it is not a question of offering our prayers
  on the basis of our own dignity
  but only on the basis of the excellence and dignity
  of Jesus Christ,
    whose righteousness is ours
      by faith.

Since the apostle for good reason
wants us to get rid of this foolish fear—
  or rather, this unbelief—
he says to us that Jesus Christ
was "made like his brothers in all things,"
  that he might be a high priest
    who is merciful and faithful
  to purify the sins of the people.[68]
For since he suffered,
being tempted,
he is also able to help those
who are tempted.[69]

And further,
to encourage us more
to approach him
he says,
"Since we have a high priest,
Jesus the Son of God,
who has entered into heaven,
we maintain our confession.
For we do not have a high priest
who is unable to have compassion for our weaknesses,
but one who was tempted in all things,
just as we are,
except for sin.
Let us go then
with confidence
to the throne of grace
that we may obtain mercy
and find grace,
in order to be helped."[70]

The same apostle says that
we "have liberty to enter into the Holy Place
by the blood of Jesus.
Let us go, then, in the assurance
of faith. . . ."[71]

Likewise
"Christ's priesthood is forever.
By this he is able to save completely
those who draw near to God through him
who always lives to intercede
for them."[72]

What more do we need?
For Christ himself declares:
"I am the way, the truth, and the life;
no one comes to my Father
but by me."[73]
Why should we seek
another intercessor?

Since it has pleased God
to give us his Son as our Intercessor,
let us not leave him for another—
    or rather seek, without ever finding.
For when God gave him to us
he knew well that we were sinners.

Therefore,
in following the command of Christ
we call on the heavenly Father
through Christ,
our only Mediator,
as we are taught by the Lord's Prayer,
    being assured that we shall obtain
    all we ask of the Father
    in his name.

[62] 1 John 2:1
[63] Phil. 2:6–8
[64] Heb. 2:17
[65] Rom. 5:10
[66] Rom. 8:34; Heb. 1:3
[67] Matt. 28:18
[68] Heb. 2:17
[69] Heb. 2:18
[70] Heb. 4:14–16
[71] Heb. 10:19, 22
[72] Heb. 7:24–25
[73] John 14:6

Article 27: *The Holy Catholic Church*

We believe and confess
one single catholic or universal church—
    a holy congregation and gathering
    of true Christian believers,
        awaiting their entire salvation in Jesus Christ
        being washed by his blood,
        and sanctified and sealed by the Holy Spirit.

This church has existed from the beginning of the world
and will last until the end,
    as appears from the fact
    that Christ is eternal King
    who cannot be without subjects.

And this holy church is preserved by God
against the rage of the whole world,
    even though for a time
    it may appear very small
    in the eyes of men—
    as though it were snuffed out.

For example,
during the very dangerous time of Ahab
the Lord preserved for himself seven thousand men
who did not bend their knees to Baal.[74]

And so this holy church
is not confined,
bound,
or limited to a certain place or certain persons.
But it is spread and dispersed
throughout the entire world,
    though still joined and united
        in heart and will,
        in one and the same Spirit,
        by the power of faith.

[74] 1 Kings 19:18

Article 28: *The Obligations of Church Members*

We believe that
    since this holy assembly and congregation
    is the gathering of those who are saved
    and there is no salvation apart from it,
no one ought to withdraw from it,
    content to be by himself,
    regardless of his status or condition.

But all people are obliged
to join and unite with it,
keeping the unity of the church
    by submitting to its instruction and discipline,
    by bending their necks under the yoke of Jesus Christ,
    and by serving to build up one another,
according to the gifts God has given them
as members of each other
in the same body.

And to preserve this unity more effectively,
it is the duty of all believers,
    according to God's Word,
to separate themselves
from those who do not belong to the church,
    in order to join this assembly
    wherever God has established it,
        even if civil authorities and royal decrees forbid
        and death and physical punishment result.

And so,
all who withdraw from the church
or do not join it
act contrary to God's ordinance.

Article 29: *The Marks of the True Church*

We believe that we ought to discern
   diligently and very carefully,
   by the Word of God,
what is the true church—
   for all sects in the world today
   claim for themselves the name of "the church."

We are not speaking here of the company of hypocrites
who are mixed among the good in the church
and who nonetheless are not part of it,
even though they are physically there.
But we are speaking of distinguishing
the body and fellowship of the true church
from all sects that call themselves "the church."

The true church can be recognized
if it has the following marks:
   The church engages in the pure preaching
      of the gospel;
   it makes use of the pure administration of the sacraments
      as Christ instituted them;
   it practices church discipline
      for correcting faults.
In short, it governs itself
according to the pure Word of God,
   rejecting all things contrary to it
   and holding Jesus Christ as the only Head.
By these marks one can be assured
of recognizing the true church—
   and no one ought to be separated from it.

As for those who can belong to the church,
we can recognize them by the distinguishing marks of Christians:
   namely by faith,
   and by their fleeing from sin and pursuing righteousness,
      once they have received the one and only Savior,
      Jesus Christ.
They love the true God and their neighbors,
   without turning to the right or left,
and they crucify the flesh and its works.

Though great weakness remains in them,
they fight against it
by the Spirit
all the days of their lives,
appealing constantly

to the blood, suffering, death, and obedience of the Lord Jesus,
   in whom they have forgiveness of their sins,
   through faith in him.

As for the false church,
it assigns more authority to itself and its ordinances
   than to the Word of God;
it does not want to subject itself
   to the yoke of Christ;
it does not administer the sacraments
   as Christ commanded in his Word;
it rather adds to them or subtracts from them
   as it pleases;
it bases itself on men,
   more than on Jesus Christ;
it persecutes those
   who live holy lives according to the Word of God
   and who rebuke it for its faults, greed, and idolatry.

These two churches
are easy to recognize
and thus to distinguish
from each other.

Article 30: *The Government of the Church*

We believe that this true church
ought to be governed according to the spiritual order
that our Lord has taught us in his Word.
   There should be ministers or pastors
      to preach the Word of God
      and adminster the sacraments.
   There should also be elders and deacons,
      along with the pastors,
      to make up the council of the church.

By this means
true religion is preserved;
true doctrine is able to take its course;
and evil men are corrected spiritually and held in check,
   so that also the poor
   and all the afflicted
   may be helped and comforted
   according to their need.

By this means
everything will be done well
and in good order

in the church,
    when such persons are elected
    who are faithful
    and are chosen according to the rule
    that Paul gave to Timothy.[75]

[75] 1 Tim. 3

Article 31: *The Officers of the Church*

We believe that
ministers of the Word of God, elders, and deacons
ought to be chosen to their offices
by a legitimate election of the church,
with prayer in the name of the Lord,
and in good order,
    as the Word of God teaches.

So everyone must be careful
not to push one's self forward improperly,
but all must wait until called by God,
    so that they may be assured of their calling
    and be certain and sure that it is
    from the Lord.

As for the ministers of the Word,
they all have the same power and authority,
    no matter where they may be,
since they are all servants of Jesus Christ,
    the only universal bishop,
    and the only head of the church.

Moreover,
to keep God's holy order
from being violated or despised,
we say that everyone ought,
as much as possible,
to hold the ministers of the Word and elders of the church
in special esteem,
    because of the work they do,
and be at peace with them,
    without grumbling, quarreling, or fighting.

Article 32: *The Order and Discipline of the Church*

We also believe that
although it is useful and good
for those who govern the churches

to establish and set up
a certain order among themselves
for maintaining the body of the church,
they ought always to guard against deviating
from what Christ,
our only Master,
has ordained
for us.

Therefore we reject all human innovations
and all laws imposed on us,
in our worship of God,
which bind and force our consciences
in any way.

So we accept only what is proper
to maintain harmony and unity
and to keep all in obedience
to God.

To that end excommunication,
with all it involves,
according to the Word of God,
is required.

Article 33: *The Sacraments*

We believe that our good God,
mindful of our crudeness and weakness,
has ordained sacraments for us
    to seal his promises in us,
    to pledge his good will and grace toward us,
    and also to nourish and sustain our faith.

He has added these to the Word of the gospel
to represent better to our external senses
both what he enables us to understand by his Word
and what he does inwardly in our hearts,
    confirming in us
    the salvation he imparts to us.

For they are visible signs and seals
of something internal and invisible,
    by means of which God works in us
    through the power of the Holy Spirit.
So they are not empty and hollow signs
to fool and deceive us,
    for their truth is Jesus Christ,
    without whom they would be nothing.

Moreover,
we are satisfied with the number of sacraments
that Christ our Master has ordained for us.
There are only two:
  the sacrament of baptism
  and the Holy Supper of Jesus Christ.

Article 34: *The Sacrament of Baptism*

We believe and confess that Jesus Christ,
in whom the law is fulfilled,
has by his shed blood
put an end to every other shedding of blood,
  which anyone might do or wish to do
  in order to atone or satisfy for sins.

Having abolished circumcision,
which was done with blood,
he established in its place
the sacrament of baptism.
  By it we are received into God's church
  and set apart from all other people and alien religions,
  that we may be dedicated entirely to him,
    bearing his mark and sign.
  It also witnesses to us
  that he will be our God forever,
    since he is our gracious Father.

Therefore he has commanded
that all those who belong to him
be baptized with pure water
  "in the name of the Father,
  and of the Son,
  and of the Holy Spirit."[76]

In this way he signifies to us
that just as water washes away the dirt of the body
when it is poured on us
and also is seen on the body of the baptized
when it is sprinkled on him,
so too the blood of Christ does the same thing internally,
in the soul,
by the Holy Spirit.
  It washes and cleanses it from its sins
  and transforms us from being the children of wrath
  into the children of God.

This does not happen by the physical water
but by the sprinkling of the precious blood of the Son of God,
who is our Red Sea,
through which we must pass
    to escape the tyranny of Pharoah,
        who is the devil,
    and to enter the spiritual land
        of Canaan.

So ministers,
as far as their work is concerned,
give us the sacrament and what is visible,
but our Lord gives what the sacrament signifies—
namely the invisible gifts and graces;
    washing, purifying, and cleansing our souls
        of all filth and unrighteousness;
    renewing our hearts and filling them
        with all comfort;
    giving us true assurance
        of his fatherly goodness;
    clothing us with the "new man" and stripping off the "old,"
        with all its works.

For this reason we believe that
anyone who aspires to reach eternal life
ought to be baptized only once
without ever repeating it—
for we cannot be born twice.
Yet this baptism is profitable
not only when the water is on us
and when we receive it
but throughout our
entire lives.

For that reason we detest the error of the Anabaptists
    who are not content with a single baptism
        once received
    and also condemn the baptism
        of the children of believers.
    We believe our children ought to be baptized
    and sealed with the sign of the covenant,
        as little children were circumcised in Israel
        on the basis of the same promises
        made to our children.

And truly,
Christ has shed his blood no less
for washing the little children of believers
than he did for adults.

Therefore they ought to receive the sign and sacrament
of what Christ has done for them,
    just as the Lord commanded in the law that
    by offering a lamb for them
    the sacrament of the suffering and death of Christ
    would be granted them
    shortly after their birth.
    This was the sacrament of Jesus Christ.

Furthermore,
baptism does for our children
what circumcision did for the Jewish people.
That is why Paul calls baptism
the "circumcision of Christ."[77]

[76] Matt. 28:19
[77] Col. 2:11

Article 35: *The Sacrament of the Lord's Supper*

We believe and confess
that our Savior Jesus Christ
has ordained and instituted the sacrament of the Holy Supper
to nourish and sustain those
who are already born again and ingrafted
into his family:
his church.

Now those who are born again have two lives in them.
The one is physical and temporal—
    they have it from the moment of their first birth,
    and it is common to all.
The other is spiritual and heavenly,
    and is given them in their second birth;
    it comes through the Word of the gospel
    in the communion of the body of Christ;
    and this life is common to God's elect only.

Thus, to support the physical and earthly life
God has prescribed for us
an appropriate earthly and material bread,
which is as common to all
as life itself also is.
But to maintain the spiritual and heavenly life
that belongs to believers
he has sent a living bread
that came down from heaven:
namely Jesus Christ,
    who nourishes and maintains

the spiritual life of believers
when eaten—
that is, when appropriated
and received spiritually
by faith.

To represent to us
this spiritual and heavenly bread
Christ has instituted
an earthly and visible bread as the sacrament of his body
and wine as the sacrament of his blood.
He did this to testify to us that
just as truly as we take and hold the sacraments in our hands
and eat and drink it in our mouths,
   by which our life is then sustained,
so truly we receive into our souls,
   for our spiritual life,
the true body and true blood of Christ,
   our only Savior.
We receive these by faith,
   which is the hand and mouth of our souls.

Now it is certain
that Jesus Christ did not prescribe
his sacraments for us in vain,
since he works in us all he represents
by these holy signs,
   although the manner in which he does it
   goes beyond our understanding
   and is incomprehensible to us,
     just as the operation of God's Spirit
     is hidden and incomprehensible.

Yet we do not go wrong when we say
that what is eaten is Christ's own natural body
and what is drunk is his own blood—
but the manner in which we eat it
is not by the mouth but by the Spirit,
through faith.

In that way Jesus Christ remains always seated
at the right hand of God his Father
in heaven—
but he never refrains on that account
to communicate himself to us
through faith.

This banquet is a spiritual table
at which Christ communicates himself to us
with all his benefits.
At that table he makes us enjoy himself
as much as the merits of his suffering and death,
as he nourishes, strengthens, and comforts
our poor, desolate souls
   by the eating of his flesh,
and relieves and renews them
   by the drinking of his blood.

Moreover,
though the sacraments and thing signified are joined together,
not all receive both of them.
The wicked person certainly takes the sacrament,
to his condemnation,
but does not receive the truth of the sacrament,
   just as Judas and Simon the Sorcerer both indeed
   received the sacrament,
   but not Christ,
   who was signified by it.
   He is communicated only to believers.

Finally,
with humility and reverence
we receive the holy sacrament
in the gathering of God's people,
   as we engage together,
   with thanksgiving,
   in a holy remembrance
   of the death of Christ our Savior,
   and as we thus confess
   our faith and Christian religion.
Therefore no one should come to this table
without examining himself carefully,
   lest "by eating this bread
   and drinking this cup
   he eat and drink to his own judgment."[78]

In short,
by the use of this holy sacrament
we are moved to a fervent love
of God and our neighbors.

Therefore we reject
as desecrations of the sacraments
all the muddled ideas and damnable inventions
that men have added and mixed in with them.

And we say that we should be content with the procedure
that Christ and the apostles have taught us
and speak of these things
as they have spoken of them.

[78] 1 Cor. 11:27

Article 36: *The Civil Government*

We believe that
because of the depravity of the human race
our good God has ordained kings, princes, and civil officers.
He wants the world to be governed by laws and policies
so that human lawlessness may be restrained
and that everything may be conducted in good order
among human beings.

For that purpose he has placed the sword
in the hands of the government,
to punish evil people
and protect the good.

And being called in this manner
to contribute to the advancement of a society
that is pleasing to God,
the civil rulers have the task,
    subject to God's law,
of removing every obstacle
    to the preaching of the gospel
    and to every aspect of divine worship.

They should do this
while completely refraining from every tendency
    toward exercising absolute authority,
and while functioning in the sphere entrusted to them,
    with the means belonging to them.

They should do it in order that
    the Word of God may have free course;
    the kingdom of Jesus Christ may make progress;
    and every anti-Christian power may be resisted.*

---

*The Synod of 1958, in line with 1910 and 1938, substituted the above statement for the following (which it
judged unbiblical): And the government's task is not limited
to caring for and watching over the public domain
but extends also to upholding the sacred ministry,
    with a view to removing and destroying
        all idolatry and false worship of the Antichrist;
    to promoting the kingdom of Jesus Christ;
    and to furthering the preaching of the gospel everywhere;
    to the end that God may be honored and served by everyone,
    as he requires in his Word.

Moreover everyone,
regardless of status, condition, or rank,
must be subject to the government,
and pay taxes,
and hold its representatives in honor and respect,
and obey them in all things that are not in conflict
    with God's Word,
praying for them
    that the Lord may be willing to lead them
        in all their ways
    and that we may live a peaceful and quiet life
        in all piety and decency.*

Article 37: *The Last Judgment*

Finally we believe,
according to God's Word,
that when the time appointed by the Lord is come
(which is unknown to all creatures)
and the number of the elect is complete,
our Lord Jesus Christ will come from heaven,
    bodily and visibly,
as he ascended,
    with great glory and majesty,
to declare himself the judge
    of the living and the dead.
He will burn this old world,
    in fire and flame,
    in order to cleanse it.

Then all human creatures will appear in person
before that great judge—
    men, women, and children,
    who have lived from the beginning until the end
    of the world.
They will be summoned there
by the voice of the archangel
and by the sound of the divine trumpet.[79]

---

*The Synod of 1985 directed that the following paragraph be taken from the body of the text and be placed in a footnote: And on this matter we denounce the Anabaptists, other anarchists,
and in general all those who want
to reject the authorities and civil officers
and to subvert justice
  by introducing common ownership of goods
  and corrupting the moral order
    that God has established among human beings.

For all those who died before that time
will be raised from the earth,
    their spirits being joined and united
    with their own bodies
    in which they lived.
And as for those who are still alive,
they will not die like the others
but will be changed "in the twinkling of an eye"
from "corruptible to incorruptible."[80]

Then "the books" (that is, the consciences) will be opened,
and the dead will be judged
    according to the things they did in the world,[81]
    whether good or evil.
Indeed, all people will give account
of all the idle words they have spoken,[82]
    which the world regards
    as only playing games.
And then the secrets and hypocrisies of men
will be publicly uncovered
in the sight of all.

Therefore,
with good reason
the thought of this judgment
is horrible and dreadful
to wicked and evil people.
But it is very pleasant
and a great comfort
to the righteous and elect,
    since their total redemption
    will then be accomplished.
They will then receive the fruits of their labor
    and of the trouble they have suffered;
their innocence will be openly recognized by all;
and they will see the terrible vengeance
    that God will bring on the evil ones
    who tyrannized, oppressed, and tormented them
        in this world.

The evil ones will be convicted
    by the witness of their own consciences,
and shall be made immortal—
    but only to be tormented
    in the everlasting fire
        prepared for the devil and his angels.[83]

In contrast,
the faithful and elect will be crowned
   with glory and honor.
The Son of God will "confess their names"[84]
   before God his Father and the holy and elect angels;
all tears will be "wiped from their eyes";[85]
and their cause—
   at present condemned as heretical and evil
   by many judges and civil officers—
will be acknowledged as the "cause of the Son of God."

And as a gracious reward
the Lord will make them possess a glory
such as the heart of man
could never imagine.

So we look forward to that great day with longing
in order to enjoy fully
the promises of God in Christ Jesus,
our Lord.

[79] 1 Thess. 4:16
[80] 1 Cor. 15:51–53
[81] Rev. 20:12
[82] Matt. 12:36
[83] Matt. 25:41
[84] Matt. 10:32
[85] Rev. 7:17

The Canons of Dort

The Decision of the Synod of Dort on the Five Main Points of Doctrine in Dispute in the Netherlands is popularly known as the *Canons of Dort*. It consists of statements of doctrine adopted by the great Synod of Dort which met in the city of Dordrecht in 1618–19. Although this was a national synod of the Reformed churches of the Netherlands, it had an international character, since it was composed not only of Dutch delegates but also of twenty-six delegates from eight foreign countries.

The Synod of Dort was held in order to settle a serious controversy in the Dutch churches initiated by the rise of Arminianism. Jacob Arminius, a theological professor at Leiden University, questioned the teaching of Calvin and his followers on a number of important points. After Arminius's death, his own followers presented their views on five of these points in the Remonstrance of 1610. In this document or in later more explicit writings, the Arminians taught election based on foreseen faith, universal atonement, partial depravity, resistible grace, and the possibility of a lapse from grace. In the Canons the Synod of Dort rejected these views and set forth the Reformed doctrine on these points, namely, unconditional election, limited atonement, total depravity, irresistible grace, and the perseverance of saints.

The Canons have a special character because of their original purpose as a judicial decision on the doctrinal points in dispute during the Arminian controversy. The original preface called them a "judgment, in which both the true view, agreeing with God's Word, concerning the aforesaid five points of doctrine is explained, and the false view, disagreeing with God's Word, is rejected." The Canons also have a limited character in that they do not cover the whole range of doctrine, but focus on the five points of doctrine in dispute.

Each of the main points consists of a positive and a negative part, the former being an exposition of the Reformed doctrine on the subject, the latter a repudiation of the corresponding errors. Each of the errors being rejected is shaded in gray. Although in form there are only four points, we speak properly of five points, because the Canons were structured to correspond to the five articles of the 1610 Remonstrance. Main Points 3 and 4 were combined into one, always designated as Main Point III/IV.

This new translation of the Canons, based on the only extant Latin manuscript among those signed at the Synod of Dort, was adopted by the 1986 Synod of the Christian Reformed Church. The biblical quotations are translations from the original Latin and so do not always correspond to current versions. Though not in the original text, subheadings have been added to the positive articles and to the conclusion in order to facilitate study of the Canons.

Formally Titled

The Decision of the Synod of Dort on the Five Main Points of Doctrine in Dispute in the Netherlands

The First Main Point of Doctrine

Divine Election and Reprobation

The Judgment Concerning Divine Predestination
Which the Synod Declares to Be in Agreement with the Word of God
and Accepted Till Now in the Reformed Churches,
Set Forth in Several Articles

Article 1: *God's Right to Condemn All People*
Since all people have sinned in Adam and have come under the sentence of the curse and eternal death, God would have done no one an injustice if it had been his will to leave the entire human race in sin and under the curse, and to condemn them on account of their sin. As the apostle says: *The whole world is liable to the condemnation of God* (Rom. 3:19), *All have sinned and are deprived of the glory of God* (Rom. 3:23), and *The wages of sin is death* (Rom. 6:23).*

Article 2: *The Manifestation of God's Love*
But this is how God showed his love: he sent his only begotten Son into the world, so that whoever believes in him should not perish but have eternal life.

Article 3: *The Preaching of the Gospel*
In order that people may be brought to faith, God mercifully sends proclaimers of this very joyful message to the people he wishes and at the time he wishes. By this ministry people are called to repentance and faith in Christ crucified. For *how shall they believe in him of whom they have not heard? And how shall they hear*

without someone preaching? And how shall they preach unless they have been sent? (Rom. 10:14–15).

Article 4: *A Twofold Response to the Gospel*
God's anger remains on those who do not believe this gospel. But those who do accept it and embrace Jesus the Savior with a true and living faith are delivered through him from God's anger and from destruction, and receive the gift of eternal life.

Article 5: *The Sources of Unbelief and of Faith*
The cause or blame for this unbelief, as well as for all other sins, is not at all in God, but in man. Faith in Jesus Christ, however, and salvation through him is a free gift of God. As Scripture says, *It is by grace you have been saved, through faith, and this not from yourselves; it is a gift of God* (Eph. 2:8). Likewise: *It has been freely given to you to believe in Christ* (Phil. 1:29).

Article 6: *God's Eternal Decision*
The fact that some receive from God the gift of faith within time, and that others do not, stems from his eternal

---

*All quotations from Scripture are translations of the original Latin manuscript.

decision. For *all his works are known to God from eternity* (Acts 15:18; Eph. 1:11). In accordance with this decision he graciously softens the hearts, however hard, of his chosen ones and inclines them to believe, but by his just judgment he leaves in their wickedness and hardness of heart those who have not been chosen. And in this especially is disclosed to us his act—unfathomable, and as merciful as it is just—of distinguishing between people equally lost. This is the well-known decision of election and reprobation revealed in God's Word. This decision the wicked, impure, and unstable distort to their own ruin, but it provides holy and godly souls with comfort beyond words.

Article 7: *Election*

Election [or choosing] is God's unchangeable purpose by which he did the following:

> Before the foundation of the world, by sheer grace, according to the free good pleasure of his will, he chose in Christ to salvation a definite number of particular people out of the entire human race, which had fallen by its own fault from its original innocence into sin and ruin. Those chosen were neither better nor more deserving than the others, but lay with them in the common misery. He did this in Christ, whom he also appointed from eternity to be the mediator, the head of all those chosen, and the foundation of their salvation.
>
> And so he decided to give the chosen ones to Christ to be saved, and to call and draw them effectively into Christ's fellowship through his Word and Spirit. In other words, he decided to grant them true faith in Christ, to justify them, to sanctify them, and finally, after powerfully preserving them in the fellowship of his Son, to glorify them.

God did all this in order to demonstrate his mercy, to the praise of the riches of his glorious grace.

As Scripture says, *God chose us in Christ, before the foundation of the world, so that we should be holy and blameless before him with love; he predestined us whom he adopted as his children through Jesus Christ, in himself, according to the good pleasure of his will, to the praise of his glorious grace, by which he freely made us pleasing to himself in his beloved* (Eph. 1:4–6). And elsewhere, *Those whom he predestined, he also called; and those whom he called, he also justified; and those whom he justified, he also glorified* (Rom. 8:30).

Article 8: *A Single Decision of Election*

This election is not of many kinds; it is one and the same election for all who were to be saved in the Old and the New Testament. For Scripture declares that there is a single good pleasure, purpose, and plan of God's will, by which he chose us from eternity both to grace and to glory, both to salvation and to the way of salvation, which he prepared in advance for us to walk in.

Article 9: *Election Not Based on Foreseen Faith*

This same election took place, not **on the basis of** foreseen faith, of the obedience of faith, of holiness, or of any other good quality and disposition, as though it were based on a prerequisite cause or condition in the person to be chosen, but rather **for the purpose of** faith, of the obedience of faith, of holiness, and so on. Accordingly, election is the source of each of the benefits of salvation. Faith, holiness, and the other saving gifts, and at last eternal life itself, flow forth from election as its fruits and effects. As the apostle says, *He chose us* (not because we were, but) *so that we should be holy and blameless before him in love* (Eph. 1:4).

Article 10: *Election Based on God's Good Pleasure*

But the cause of this undeserved election is exclusively the good pleasure of God. This does not involve his choosing certain human qualities or actions from among all those possible as a condition of salvation, but rather involves his adopting certain particular persons from among the common mass of sinners as his own possession. As Scripture says, *When the children were not yet born, and had done nothing either good or bad. . . , she* (Rebecca) *was told, "The older will serve the younger." As it is written, "Jacob I loved, but Esau I hated"* (Rom. 9:11–13). Also, *All who were appointed for eternal life believed* (Acts 13:48).

Article 11: *Election Unchangeable*

Just as God himself is most wise, unchangeable, all-knowing, and almighty, so the election made by him can neither be suspended nor altered, revoked, or annulled; neither can his chosen ones be cast off, nor their number reduced.

Article 12: *The Assurance of Election*

Assurance of this their eternal and unchangeable election to salvation is given to the chosen in due time, though by various stages and in differing measure. Such assurance comes not by inquisitive searching into the hidden and deep things of God, but by noticing within themselves, with spiritual joy and holy delight, the unmistakable fruits of election pointed out in God's Word—such as a true faith in Christ, a childlike fear of God, a godly sorrow for their sins, a hunger and thirst for righteousness, and so on.

Article 13: *The Fruit of This Assurance*

In their awareness and assurance of this election God's children daily find greater cause to humble themselves before God, to adore the fathomless depth of his mercies, to cleanse themselves, and to give fervent love in return to him who first so greatly loved them. This is far from saying that this teaching concerning election, and reflection upon it, make God's children lax in observing his commandments or carnally self-assured. By God's just judgment this does usually happen to those who casually take for granted the grace of election or engage in idle and brazen talk about it but are unwilling to walk in the ways of the chosen.

Article 14: *Teaching Election Properly*

Just as, by God's wise plan, this teaching concerning divine election has been proclaimed through the prophets, Christ himself, and the apostles, in Old and New Testament times, and has subsequently been committed to writing in the Holy Scriptures, so also today in God's church, for which it was specifically intended, this teaching must be set forth—with a spirit of discretion, in a godly and holy manner, at the appropriate time and place, without inquisitive searching into the ways of the Most High. This must be done for the glory of God's most holy name, and for the lively comfort of his people.

Article 15: *Reprobation*

Moreover, Holy Scripture most especially highlights this eternal and undeserved grace of our election and brings it out more clearly for us, in that it further bears witness that not all people have been chosen but that some have not been chosen or have been passed by in God's eternal election—those, that is, concerning whom God, on the basis of his entirely free, most just, irreproachable, and unchangeable good pleasure, made the following decision:

> to leave them in the common misery into which, by their own fault, they have plunged themselves;
> not to grant them saving faith and the grace of conversion;
> but finally to condemn and eternally punish them (having been left in their own ways and under his just judgment), not only for their unbelief but also for all their other sins, in order to display his justice.

And this is the decision of reprobation, which does not at all make God the author of sin (a blasphemous thought!) but rather its fearful, irreproachable, just judge and avenger.

Article 16: *Responses to the Teaching of Reprobation*
Those who do not yet actively experience within themselves a living faith in Christ or an assured confidence of heart, peace of conscience, a zeal for childlike obedience, and a glorying in God through Christ, but who nevertheless use the means by which God has promised to work these things in us— such people ought not to be alarmed at the mention of reprobation, nor to count themselves among the reprobate; rather they ought to continue diligently in the use of the means, to desire fervently a time of more abundant grace, and to wait for it in reverence and humility. On the other hand, those who seriously desire to turn to God, to be pleasing to him alone,

and to be delivered from the body of death, but are not yet able to make such progress along the way of godliness and faith as they would like—such people ought much less to stand in fear of the teaching concerning reprobation, since our merciful God has promised that he will not snuff out a smoldering wick and that he will not break a bruised reed. However, those who have forgotten God and their Savior Jesus Christ and have abandoned themselves wholly to the cares of the world and the pleasures of the flesh—such people have every reason to stand in fear of this teaching, as long as they do not seriously turn to God.

Article 17: *The Salvation of the Infants of Believers*
Since we must make judgments about God's will from his Word, which testifies that the children of believers are holy, not by nature but by virtue of the gracious covenant in which they together with their parents are included, godly parents ought not to doubt the election and salvation of their children whom God calls out of this life in infancy.

Article 18: *The Proper Attitude Toward Election and Reprobation*
To those who complain about this grace of an undeserved election and about the severity of a just reprobation, we reply with the words of the apostle, *Who are you, O man, to talk back to God?* (Rom. 9:20), and with the words of our Savior, *Have I no right to do what I want with my own?* (Matt. 20:15). We, however, with reverent adoration of these secret things, cry out with the apostle: *Oh, the depths of the riches both of the wisdom and the knowledge of God! How unsearchable are his judgments, and his ways beyond tracing out! For who has known the mind of the Lord? Or who has been his counselor? Or who has first given to God, that*

God should repay him? For from him and through him and to him are all things. To him be the glory forever! Amen (Rom. 11:33–36).

*Rejection of the Errors
by Which the Dutch Churches
Have for Some Time Been Disturbed*

Having set forth the orthodox teaching concerning election and reprobation, the Synod rejects the errors of those

I

Who teach that the will of God to save those who would believe and persevere in faith and in the obedience of faith is the whole and entire decision of election to salvation, and that nothing else concerning this decision has been revealed in God's Word.

For they deceive the simple and plainly contradict Holy Scripture in its testimony that God does not only wish to save those who would believe, but that he has also from eternity chosen certain particular people to whom, rather than to others, he would within time grant faith in Christ and perseverance. As Scripture says, *I have revealed your name to those whom you gave me* (John 17:6). Likewise, *All who were appointed for eternal life believed* (Acts 13:48), and *He chose us before the foundation of the world so that we should be holy. . .* (Eph. 1:4).

II

Who teach that God's election to eternal life is of many kinds: one general and indefinite, the other particular and definite; and the latter in turn either incomplete, revocable, nonperemptory (or conditional), or else complete, irrevocable, and peremptory (or absolute). Likewise, who teach that there is one election to faith and another to salvation, so that there can be an election to justifying faith apart from a peremptory election to salvation.

For this is an invention of the human brain, devised apart from the Scriptures, which distorts the teaching concerning election and breaks up this golden chain of salvation: *Those whom he predestined, he also called; and those whom he called, he also justified; and those whom he justified, he also glorified* (Rom. 8:30).

III

Who teach that God's good pleasure and purpose, which Scripture mentions in its teaching of election, does not involve God's choosing certain particular people rather than others, but involves God's choosing, out of all possible conditions (including the works of the law) or out of the whole order of things, the intrinsically unworthy act of faith, as well as the imperfect obedience of faith, to be a condition of salvation; and it involves his graciously wishing to count this as perfect obedience and to look upon it as worthy of the reward of eternal life.

For by this pernicious error the good pleasure of God and the merit of Christ are robbed of their effectiveness and people are drawn away, by unprofitable inquiries, from the truth of undeserved justification and from the simplicity of the Scriptures. It also gives the lie to these words of the apostle: *God called us with a holy calling, not in virtue of works, but in virtue of his own purpose and the grace which was given to us in Christ Jesus before the beginning of time* (2 Tim. 1:9).

IV

Who teach that in election to faith a prerequisite condition is that man should rightly use the light of nature, be upright, unassuming, humble, and disposed to eternal life, as though election depended to some extent on these factors.

For this smacks of Pelagius, and it clearly calls into question the words of the apostle: *We lived at one time in the passions of our flesh, following the will of our flesh and thoughts, and we were by nature children of wrath, like everyone else. But God, who is rich in mercy, out of the great love with which he loved us, even when we were dead in transgressions, made us alive with Christ, by whose grace you have been saved. And God raised us up with him and seated us with him in heaven in Christ Jesus, in order that in the coming ages we might show the surpassing riches of his grace, according to his kindness toward us in Christ Jesus. For it is by grace you have been saved, through faith (and this not from yourselves; it is the gift of God) not by works, so that no one can boast* (Eph. 2:3–9).

V

Who teach that the incomplete and nonperemptory election of particular persons to salvation occurred on the basis of a foreseen faith, repentance, holiness, and godliness, which has just begun or continued for some time; but that complete and peremptory election occurred on the basis of a foreseen perseverance to the end in faith, repentance, holiness, and godliness. And that this is the gracious and evangelical worthiness, on account of which the one who is chosen is more worthy than the one who is not chosen. And therefore that faith, the obedience of faith, holiness, godliness, and perseverance are not fruits or effects of an unchangeable election to glory, but indispensable conditions and causes, which are prerequisite in those who are to be chosen in the complete election, and which are foreseen as achieved in them.

This runs counter to the entire Scripture, which throughout impresses upon our ears and hearts these sayings among others: *Election is not by works, but by him who calls* (Rom. 9:11–12); *All who were appointed for eternal life believed* (Acts 13:48); *He chose us in himself so that we should be holy* (Eph. 1:4); *You did not choose me, but I chose you* (John 15:16); *If by grace, not by works* (Rom. 11:6); *In this is love, not that we loved God, but that he loved us and sent his Son* (1 John 4:10).

VI

Who teach that not every election to salvation is unchangeable, but that some of the chosen can perish and do in fact perish eternally, with no decision of God to prevent it.

By this gross error they make God changeable, destroy the comfort of the godly concerning the steadfastness of their election, and contradict the Holy Scriptures, which teach that *the elect cannot be led astray* (Matt. 24:24), that *Christ does not lose those given to him by the Father* (John 6:39), and that *those whom God predestined, called, and justified, he also glorifies* (Rom. 8:30).

VII

Who teach that in this life there is no fruit, no awareness, and no assurance of one's unchangeable election to glory, except as conditional upon something changeable and contingent.

For not only is it absurd to speak of an uncertain assurance, but these things also militate against the experience of the saints, who with the apostle rejoice from an awareness of their election and sing the praises of this gift of God; who, as Christ urged, *rejoice* with his disciples *that their names have been written in heaven* (Luke 10:20); and finally who hold up against the flaming arrows of the devil's temptations the awareness of their election, with the question *Who will bring any charge against those whom God has chosen?* (Rom. 8:33).

VIII

Who teach that it was not on the basis of his just will alone that God decided to leave anyone in the fall of Adam and in the common state of sin and condemnation or to pass anyone by in the imparting of grace necessary for faith and conversion.

For these words stand fast: *He has mercy on whom he wishes, and he hardens whom he wishes* (Rom. 9:18). And also: *To you it has been given to know the secrets of the kingdom of heaven, but to them it has not been given* (Matt. 13:11). Likewise: *I give glory to you, Father, Lord of heaven and earth, that you have hidden these things from the wise and understanding, and have revealed them to little children; yes, Father, because that was your pleasure* (Matt. 11:25–26).

IX

Who teach that the cause for God's sending the gospel to one people rather than to another is not merely and solely God's good pleasure, but rather that one people is better and worthier than the other to whom the gospel is not communicated.

For Moses contradicts this when he addresses the people of Israel as follows: *Behold, to Jehovah your God belong the heavens and the highest heavens, the earth and whatever is in it. But Jehovah was inclined in his affection to love your ancestors alone, and chose out their descendants after them, you above all peoples, as at this day* (Deut. 10:14–15). And also Christ: *Woe to you, Korazin! Woe to you, Bethsaida! for if those mighty works done in you had been done in Tyre and Sidon, they would have repented long ago in sackcloth and ashes* (Matt. 11:21).

The Second Main Point of Doctrine

Christ's Death and Human Redemption Through It

Article 1: *The Punishment Which God's Justice Requires*

God is not only supremely merciful, but also supremely just. His justice requires (as he has revealed himself in the Word) that the sins we have committed against his infinite majesty be punished with both temporal and eternal punishments, of soul as well as body. We cannot escape these punishments unless satisfaction is given to God's justice.

Article 2: *The Satisfaction Made by Christ*

Since, however, we ourselves cannot give this satisfaction or deliver ourselves from God's anger, God in his boundless mercy has given us as a guarantee his only begotten Son, who was made to be sin and a curse for us, in our place, on the cross, in order that he might give satisfaction for us.

Article 3: *The Infinite Value of Christ's Death*

This death of God's Son is the only and entirely complete sacrifice and satisfaction for sins; it is of infinite value and worth, more than sufficient to atone for the sins of the whole world.

Article 4: *Reasons for This Infinite Value*

This death is of such great value and worth for the reason that the person who suffered it is—as was necessary to be our Savior—not only a true and perfectly holy man, but also the only begotten Son of God, of the same eternal and infinite essence with the Father and the Holy Spirit. Another reason is that this death was accompanied by the experience of God's anger and curse, which **we** by our sins had fully deserved.

Article 5: *The Mandate to Proclaim the Gospel to All*

Moreover, it is the promise of the gospel that whoever believes in Christ crucified shall not perish but have eternal life. This promise, together with the command to repent and believe, ought to be announced and declared without differentiation or discrimination to all nations and people, to whom God in his good pleasure sends the gospel.

Article 6: *Unbelief Man's Responsibility*

However, that many who have been called through the gospel do not repent or believe in Christ but perish in unbelief is not because the sacrifice of Christ offered on the cross is deficient or insufficient, but because they themselves are at fault.

Article 7: *Faith God's Gift*

But all who genuinely believe and are delivered and saved by Christ's death from their sins and from destruction receive this favor solely from God's grace—which he owes to no one—given to them in Christ from eternity.

Article 8: *The Saving Effectiveness of Christ's Death*

For it was the entirely free plan and very gracious will and intention of God the Father that the enlivening and saving effectiveness of his Son's costly death should work itself out in all his chosen ones, in order that he might grant justifying faith to them only and thereby lead them without fail to salvation. In other words, it was God's will that Christ through the blood of the cross (by which he confirmed the new covenant) should effectively redeem from every people, tribe, nation, and language all those and only those who were chosen from eternity to salvation and given to him by the Father; that he should grant them faith (which, like the Holy Spirit's other saving gifts, he acquired for them by his death); that he should cleanse them by his blood from all their sins, both original and actual, whether committed before or after their coming to faith; that he should faithfully preserve them to the very end; and that he should finally present them to himself, a glorious people, without spot or wrinkle.

Article 9: *The Fulfillment of God's Plan*

This plan, arising out of God's eternal love for his chosen ones, from the beginning of the world to the present time has been powerfully carried out and will also be carried out in the future, the gates of hell seeking vainly to prevail against it. As a result the chosen are gathered into one, all in their own time, and there is always a church of believers founded on Christ's blood, a church which steadfastly loves, persistently worships, and—here and in all eternity—praises him as her Savior who laid down his life for her on the cross, as a bridegroom for his bride.

Rejection of the Errors

Having set forth the orthodox teaching, the Synod rejects the errors of those

I

Who teach that God the Father appointed his Son to death on the cross without a fixed and definite plan to save anyone by name, so that the necessity, usefulness, and worth of what Christ's death obtained could have stood intact and altogether perfect, complete and whole, even if the redemption that was obtained had never in actual fact been applied to any individual.

For this assertion is an insult to the wisdom of God the Father and to the merit of Jesus Christ, and it is contrary to Scripture. For the Savior speaks as follows: *I lay down my life for the sheep, and I know them* (John 10:15, 27). And Isaiah the prophet says concerning the Savior: *When he shall make himself an offering for sin, he shall see his offspring, he shall prolong his days, and the will of Jehovah shall prosper in his hand* (Isa. 53:10). Finally, this undermines the article of the creed in which we confess what we believe concerning the church.

II

Who teach that the purpose of Christ's death was not to establish in actual fact a new covenant of grace by his blood, but only to acquire for the Father the mere right to enter once more into a covenant with men, whether of grace or of works.

For this conflicts with Scripture, which teaches that Christ *has become the guarantee and mediator of a better*—that is, *a new*—*covenant* (Heb. 7:22; 9:15), and that *a will is in force only when someone has died* (Heb. 9:17).

III

Who teach that Christ, by the satisfaction which he gave, did not certainly merit for anyone salvation itself and the faith by which this satisfaction of Christ is effectively applied to salvation, but only acquired for the Father the authority or plenary will to relate in a new way with men and to impose such new conditions as he chose, and that the satisfying of these conditions depends on the free choice of man; consequently, that it was possible that either all or none would fulfill them.

For they have too low an opinion of the death of Christ, do not at all acknowledge the foremost fruit or benefit which it brings forth, and summon back from hell the Pelagian error.

IV

Who teach that what is involved in the new covenant of grace which God the Father made with men through the intervening of Christ's death is not that we are justified before God and saved through faith, insofar as it accepts Christ's merit, but rather that God, having withdrawn his demand for perfect obedience to the law, counts faith itself, and the imperfect obedience of faith, as perfect obedience to the law, and graciously looks upon this as worthy of the reward of eternal life.

For they contradict Scripture: *They are justified freely by his grace through the redemption that came by Jesus Christ, whom God presented as a sacrifice of atonement, through faith in his blood* (Rom. 3:24–25). And along with the ungodly Socinus, they introduce a new and foreign justification of man before God, against the consensus of the whole church.

V

Who teach that all people have been received into the state of reconciliation and into the grace of the covenant, so that no one on account of original sin is liable to condemnation, or is to be condemned, but that all are free from the guilt of this sin.

For this opinion conflicts with Scripture which asserts that we are by nature children of wrath.

VI

Who make use of the distinction between obtaining and applying in order to instill in the unwary and inexperienced the opinion that God, as far as he is concerned, wished to bestow equally upon all people the benefits which are gained by Christ's death; but that the distinction by which some rather than others come to share in the forgiveness of sins and eternal life depends on their own free choice (which applies itself to the grace offered indiscriminately) but does not depend on the unique gift of mercy which effectively works in them, so that they, rather than others, apply that grace to themselves.

For, while pretending to set forth this distinction in an acceptable sense, they attempt to give the people the deadly poison of Pelagianism.

VII

Who teach that Christ neither could die, nor had to die, nor did die for those whom God so dearly loved and chose to eternal life, since such people do not need the death of Christ.

For they contradict the apostle, who says: *Christ loved me and gave himself up for me* (Gal. 2:20), and likewise: *Who will bring any charge against those whom God has chosen? It is God who justifies. Who is he that condemns? It is Christ who died,* that is, for them (Rom. 8:33–34). They also contradict the Savior, who asserts: *I lay down my life for the sheep* (John 10:15), and *My command is this: Love one another as I have loved you. Greater love has no one than this, that one lay down his life for his friends* (John 15:12–13).

The Third and Fourth Main Points of Doctrine

Human Corruption, Conversion to God, and the Way It Occurs

Article 1: *The Effect of the Fall on Human Nature*

Man was originally created in the image of God and was furnished in his mind with a true and salutary knowledge of his Creator and things spiritual, in his will and heart with righteousness, and in all his emotions with purity; indeed, the whole man was holy. However, rebelling against God at the devil's instigation and by his own free will, he deprived himself of these outstanding gifts. Rather, in their place he brought upon himself blindness, terrible darkness, futility, and distortion of judgment in his mind; perversity, defiance, and hardness in his heart and will; and finally impurity in all his emotions.

Article 2: *The Spread of Corruption*

Man brought forth children of the same nature as himself after the fall. That is to say, being corrupt he brought forth corrupt children. The corruption spread, by God's just judgment, from Adam to all his descendants—except for Christ alone—not by way of imitation (as in former times the Pelagians would have it) but by way of the propagation of his perverted nature.

Article 3: *Total Inability*

Therefore, all people are conceived in sin and are born children of wrath, unfit for any saving good, inclined to evil, dead in their sins, and slaves to sin; without the grace of the regenerating Holy Spirit they are neither willing nor able to return to God, to reform their distorted nature, or even to dispose themselves to such reform.

Article 4: *The Inadequacy of the Light of Nature*

There is, to be sure, a certain light of nature remaining in man after the fall, by virtue of which he retains some notions about God, natural things, and the difference between what is moral and immoral, and demonstrates a certain eagerness for virtue and for good outward behavior. But this light of nature is far from enabling man to come to a saving knowledge of God and conversion to him—so far, in fact, that man does not use it rightly even in matters of nature and society. Instead, in various ways he completely distorts this light, whatever its precise character, and suppresses it in unrighteousness. In doing so he renders himself without excuse before God.

Article 5: *The Inadequacy of the Law*

In this respect, what is true of the light of nature is true also of the Ten Commandments given by God through Moses specifically to the Jews. For man cannot obtain saving grace through the Decalogue, because, although it does expose the magnitude of his sin and increasingly convict him of his guilt, yet it does not offer a remedy or enable him to escape from his misery, and, indeed, weakened as it is by the flesh, leaves the offender under the curse.

Article 6: *The Saving Power of the Gospel*

What, therefore, neither the light of nature nor the law can do, God accomplishes by the power of the Holy Spirit, through the Word or the ministry of reconciliation. This is the gospel about the Messiah, through which it has pleased God to save believers, in both the Old and the New Testament.

Article 7: *God's Freedom in Revealing the Gospel*
In the Old Testament, God revealed this secret of his will to a small number; in the New Testament (now without any distinction between peoples) he discloses it to a large number. The reason for this difference must not be ascribed to the greater worth of one nation over another, or to a better use of the light of nature, but to the free good pleasure and undeserved love of God. Therefore, those who receive so much grace, beyond and in spite of all they deserve, ought to acknowledge it with humble and thankful hearts; on the other hand, with the apostle they ought to adore (but certainly not inquisitively search into) the severity and justice of God's judgments on the others, who do not receive this grace.

Article 8: *The Serious Call of the Gospel*
Nevertheless, all who are called through the gospel are called seriously. For seriously and most genuinely God makes known in his Word what is pleasing to him: that those who are called should come to him. Seriously he also promises rest for their souls and eternal life to all who come to him and believe.

Article 9: *Human Responsibility for Rejecting the Gospel*
The fact that many who are called through the ministry of the gospel do not come and are not brought to conversion must not be blamed on the gospel, nor on Christ, who is offered through the gospel, nor on God, who calls them through the gospel and even bestows various gifts on them, but on the people themselves who are called. Some in self-assurance do not even entertain the Word of life; others do

entertain it but do not take it to heart, and for that reason, after the fleeting joy of a temporary faith, they relapse; others choke the seed of the Word with the thorns of life's cares and with the pleasures of the world and bring forth no fruits. This our Savior teaches in the parable of the sower (Matt. 13).

Article 10: *Conversion as the Work of God*
The fact that others who are called through the ministry of the gospel do come and are brought to conversion must not be credited to man, as though one distinguishes himself by free choice from others who are furnished with equal or sufficient grace for faith and conversion (as the proud heresy of Pelagius maintains). No, it must be credited to God: just as from eternity he chose his own in Christ, so within time he effectively calls them, grants them faith and repentance, and, having rescued them from the dominion of darkness, brings them into the kingdom of his Son, in order that they may declare the wonderful deeds of him who called them out of darkness into this marvelous light, and may boast not in themselves, but in the Lord, as apostolic words frequently testify in Scripture.

Article 11: *The Holy Spirit's Work in Conversion*
Moreover, when God carries out this good pleasure in his chosen ones, or works true conversion in them, he not only sees to it that the gospel is proclaimed to them outwardly, and enlightens their minds powerfully by the Holy Spirit so that they may rightly understand and discern the things of the Spirit of God, but, by the effective operation of the same regenerating Spirit, he also penetrates into the inmost being of man, opens the closed heart, softens the hard heart, and circumcises the heart

that is uncircumcised. He infuses new qualities into the will, making the dead will alive, the evil one good, the unwilling one willing, and the stubborn one compliant; he activates and strengthens the will so that, like a good tree, it may be enabled to produce the fruits of good deeds.

Article 12: *Regeneration a Supernatural Work*

And this is the regeneration, the new creation, the raising from the dead, and the making alive so clearly proclaimed in the Scriptures, which God works in us without our help. But this certainly does not happen only by outward teaching, by moral persuasion, or by such a way of working that, after God has done his work, it remains in man's power whether or not to be reborn or converted. Rather, it is an entirely supernatural work, one that is at the same time most powerful and most pleasing, a marvelous, hidden, and inexpressible work, which is not lesser than or inferior in power to that of creation or of raising the dead, as Scripture (inspired by the author of this work) teaches. As a result, all those in whose hearts God works in this marvelous way are certainly, unfailingly, and effectively reborn and do actually believe. And then the will, now renewed, is not only activated and motivated by God but in being activated by God is also itself active. For this reason, man himself, by that grace which he has received, is also rightly said to believe and to repent.

Article 13: *The Incomprehensible Way of Regeneration*

In this life believers cannot fully understand the way this work occurs; meanwhile, they rest content with knowing and experiencing that by this grace of God they do believe with the heart and love their Savior.

Article 14: *The Way God Gives Faith*

In this way, therefore, faith is a gift of God, not in the sense that it is offered by God for man to choose, but that it is in actual fact bestowed on man, breathed and infused into him. Nor is it a gift in the sense that God bestows only the potential to believe, but then awaits assent—the act of believing—from man's choice; rather, it is a gift in the sense that he who works both willing and acting and, indeed, works all things in all people produces in man both the will to believe and the belief itself.

Article 15: *Responses to God's Grace*

God does not owe this grace to anyone. For what could God owe to one who has nothing to give that can be paid back? Indeed, what could God owe to one who has nothing of his own to give but sin and falsehood? Therefore the person who receives this grace owes and gives eternal thanks to God alone; the person who does not receive it either does not care at all about these spiritual things and is satisfied with himself in his condition, or else in self-assurance foolishly boasts about having something which he lacks. Furthermore, following the example of the apostles, we are to think and to speak in the most favorable way about those who outwardly profess their faith and better their lives, for the inner chambers of the heart are unknown to us. But for others who have not yet been called, we are to pray to the God who calls things that do not exist as though they did. In no way, however, are we to pride ourselves as better than they, as though we had distinguished ourselves from them.

Article 16: *Regeneration's Effect*

However, just as by the fall man did not cease to be man, endowed with intellect and will, and just as sin, which has spread through the whole human race, did not abolish the nature of the human race but distorted and spiritually killed it, so also this divine grace of regeneration does not act in people as if they were blocks and stones; nor does it abolish the will and its properties or coerce a reluctant will by force, but spiritually revives, heals, reforms, and—in a manner at once pleasing and powerful—bends it back. As a result, a ready and sincere obedience of the Spirit now begins to prevail where before the rebellion and resistance of the flesh were completely dominant. It is in this that the true and spiritual restoration and freedom of our will consists. Thus, if the marvelous Maker of every good thing were not dealing with us, man would have no hope of getting up from his fall by his free choice, by which he plunged himself into ruin when still standing upright.

Article 17: *God's Use of Means in Regeneration*

Just as the almighty work of God by which he brings forth and sustains our natural life does not rule out but requires the use of means, by which God, according to his infinite wisdom and goodness, has wished to exercise his power, so also the aforementioned supernatural work of God by which he regenerates us in no way rules out or cancels the use of the gospel, which God in his great wisdom has appointed to be the seed of regeneration and the food of the soul. For this reason, the apostles and the teachers who followed them taught the people in a godly manner about this grace of God, to give him the glory and to humble all pride, and yet did not neglect meanwhile to keep the people, by means of the holy admonitions of the gospel, under the administration of the Word, the sacraments, and discipline. So even today it is out of the question that the teachers

or those taught in the church should presume to test God by separating what he in his good pleasure has wished to be closely joined together. For grace is bestowed through admonitions, and the more readily we perform our duty, the more lustrous the benefit of God working in us usually is and the better his work advances. To him alone, both for the means and for their saving fruit and effectiveness, all glory is owed forever. Amen.

Rejection of the Errors

Having set forth the orthodox teaching, the Synod rejects the errors of those

I

Who teach that, properly speaking, it cannot be said that original sin in itself is enough to condemn the whole human race or to warrant temporal and eternal punishments.

For they contradict the apostle when he says: *Sin entered the world through one man, and death through sin, and in this way death passed on to all men because all sinned* (Rom. 5:12); also: *The guilt followed one sin and brought condemnation* (Rom. 5:16); likewise: *The wages of sin is death* (Rom. 6:23).

II

Who teach that the spiritual gifts or the good dispositions and virtues such as goodness, holiness, and righteousness could not have resided in man's will when he was first created, and therefore could not have been separated from the will at the fall.

For this conflicts with the apostle's description of the image of God in Ephesians 4:24, where he portrays the image in terms of righteousness and holiness, which definitely reside in the will.

III

Who teach that in spiritual death the spiritual gifts have not been separated from man's will, since the will in itself has never been corrupted but only hindered by the darkness of the mind and the unruliness of the emotions, and since the will is able to exercise its innate free capacity once these hindrances are removed, which is to say, it is able of itself to will or choose whatever good is set before it—or else not to will or choose it.

This is a novel idea and an error and has the effect of elevating the power of free choice, contrary to the words of Jeremiah the prophet: *The heart itself is deceitful above all things and wicked* (Jer. 17:9); and of the words of the apostle: *All of us also lived among them* (the sons of disobedience) *at one time in the passions of our flesh, following the will of our flesh and thoughts* (Eph. 2:3).

IV

Who teach that unregenerate man is not strictly or totally dead in his sins or deprived of all capacity for spiritual good but is able to hunger and thirst for righteousness or life and to offer the sacrifice of a broken and contrite spirit which is pleasing to God.

For these views are opposed to the plain testimonies of Scripture: *You were dead in your transgressions and sins* (Eph. 2:1, 5); *The imagination of the thoughts of man's heart is only evil all the time* (Gen. 6:5; 8:21). Besides, to hunger and thirst for deliverance from misery and for life, and to offer God the sacrifice of a broken spirit is characteristic only of the regenerate and of those called blessed (Ps. 51:17; Matt. 5:6).

V

Who teach that corrupt and natural man can make such good use of common grace (by which they mean the light of nature) or of the gifts remaining after the fall that he is able thereby gradually to obtain a greater grace—evangelical or saving grace—as well as salvation itself; and that in this way God, for his part, shows himself ready to reveal Christ to all people, since he provides to all, to a sufficient extent and in an effective manner, the means necessary for the revealing of Christ, for faith, and for repentance.

For Scripture, not to mention the experience of all ages, testifies that this is false: *He makes known his words to Jacob, his statutes and his laws to Israel; he has done this for no other nation, and they do not know his laws* (Ps. 147:19–20); *In the past God let all nations go their own way* (Acts 14:16); *They* (Paul and his companions) *were kept by the Holy Spirit from speaking God's word in Asia;* and *When they had come to Mysia, they tried to go to Bithynia, but the Spirit would not allow them to* (Acts 16:6–7).

VI

Who teach that in the true conversion of man new qualities, dispositions, or gifts cannot be infused or poured into his will by God, and indeed that the faith [or believing] by which we first come to conversion and from which we receive the name "believers" is not a quality or gift infused by God, but only an act of man, and that it cannot be called a gift except in respect to the power of attaining faith.

For these views contradict the Holy Scriptures, which testify that God does infuse or pour into our hearts the new qualities of faith, obedience, and the experiencing of his love: *I will put my law in their minds, and write it on their hearts*

(Jer. 31:33); *I will pour water on the thirsty land, and streams on the dry ground; I will pour out my Spirit on your offspring* (Isa. 44:3); *The love of God has been poured out in our hearts by the Holy Spirit, who has been given to us* (Rom. 5:5). They also conflict with the continuous practice of the Church, which prays with the prophet: *Convert me, Lord, and I shall be converted* (Jer. 31:18).

VII

Who teach that the grace by which we are converted to God is nothing but a gentle persuasion, or (as others explain it) that the way of God's acting in man's conversion that is most noble and suited to human nature is that which happens by persuasion, and that nothing prevents this grace of moral suasion even by itself from making natural men spiritual; indeed, that God does not produce the assent of the will except in this manner of moral suasion, and that the effectiveness of God's work by which it surpasses the work of Satan consists in the fact that God promises eternal benefits while Satan promises temporal ones.

For this teaching is entirely Pelagian and contrary to the whole of Scripture, which recognizes besides this persuasion also another, far more effective and divine way in which the Holy Spirit acts in man's conversion. As Ezekiel 36:26 puts it: *I will give you a new heart and put a new spirit in you; and I will remove your heart of stone and give you a heart of flesh. . . .*

VIII

Who teach that God in regenerating man does not bring to bear that power of his omnipotence whereby he may powerfully and unfailingly bend man's will to faith and conversion, but that even when God has accomplished all the works of grace which he uses for man's conversion, man nevertheless can, and in actual fact often does, so resist God and the Spirit in their intent and will to regenerate him, that man completely thwarts his own rebirth; and, indeed, that it remains in his own power whether or not to be reborn.

For this does away with all effective functioning of God's grace in our conversion and subjects the activity of Almighty God to the will of man; it is contrary to the apostles, who teach that *we believe by virtue of the effective working of God's mighty strength* (Eph. 1:19), and that *God fulfills the undeserved good will of his kindness and the work of faith in us with power* (2 Thess. 1:11), and likewise that *his divine power has given us everything we need for life and godliness* (2 Pet. 1:3).

IX

Who teach that grace and free choice are concurrent partial causes which cooperate to initiate conversion, and that grace does not precede—in the order of causality—the effective influence of the will; that is to say, that God does not effectively help man's will to come to conversion before man's will itself motivates and determines itself.

For the early church already condemned this doctrine long ago in the Pelagians, on the basis of the words of the apostle: *It does not depend on man's willing or running but on God's mercy* (Rom. 9:16); also: *Who makes you different from anyone else?* and *What do you have that you did not receive?* (1 Cor. 4:7); likewise: *It is God who works in you to will and act according to his good pleasure* (Phil. 2:13).

The Fifth Main Point of Doctrine

The Perseverance of the Saints

Article 1: *The Regenerate Not Entirely Free from Sin*

Those people whom God according to his purpose calls into fellowship with his Son Jesus Christ our Lord and regenerates by the Holy Spirit, he also sets free from the reign and slavery of sin, though in this life not entirely from the flesh and from the body of sin.

Article 2: *The Believer's Reaction to Sins of Weakness*

Hence daily sins of weakness arise, and blemishes cling to even the best works of God's people, giving them continual cause to humble themselves before God, to flee for refuge to Christ crucified, to put the flesh to death more and more by the Spirit of supplication and by holy exercises of godliness, and to strain toward the goal of perfection, until they are freed from this body of death and reign with the Lamb of God in heaven.

Article 3: *God's Preservation of the Converted*

Because of these remnants of sin dwelling in them and also because of the temptations of the world and Satan, those who have been converted could not remain standing in this grace if left to their own resources. But God is faithful, mercifully strengthening them in the grace once conferred on them and powerfully preserving them in it to the end.

Article 4: *The Danger of True Believers' Falling into Serious Sins*

Although that power of God strengthening and preserving true believers in grace is more than a match for the flesh, yet those converted are not always so activated and motivated by God that in certain specific actions they cannot by their own fault depart from the leading of grace, be led astray by the desires of the flesh, and give in to them. For this reason they must constantly watch and pray that they may not be led into temptations. When they fail to do this, not only **can** they be carried away by the flesh, the world, and Satan into sins, even serious and outrageous ones, but also by God's just permission they sometimes **are** so carried away—witness the sad cases, described in Scripture, of David, Peter, and other saints falling into sins.

Article 5: *The Effects of Such Serious Sins*

By such monstrous sins, however, they greatly offend God, deserve the sentence of death, grieve the Holy Spirit, suspend the exercise of faith, severely wound the conscience, and sometimes lose the awareness of grace for a time—until, after they have returned to the way by genuine repentance, God's fatherly face again shines upon them.

Article 6: *God's Saving Intervention*

For God, who is rich in mercy, according to his unchangeable purpose of election does not take his Holy Spirit from his own completely, even when they fall grievously. Neither does he let them fall down so far that they forfeit the grace of adoption and the state of justification, or commit the sin which leads to death (the sin against the Holy Spirit), and plunge themselves, entirely forsaken by him, into eternal ruin.

Article 7: *Renewal to Repentance*

For, in the first place, God preserves

in those saints when they fall his imperishable seed from which they have been born again, lest it perish or be dislodged. Secondly, by his Word and Spirit he certainly and effectively renews them to repentance so that they have a heartfelt and godly sorrow for the sins they have committed; seek and obtain, through faith and with a contrite heart, forgiveness in the blood of the Mediator; experience again the grace of a reconciled God; through faith adore his mercies; and from then on more eagerly work out their own salvation with fear and trembling.

Article 8: *The Certainty of This Preservation*

So it is not by their own merits or strength but by God's undeserved mercy that they neither forfeit faith and grace totally nor remain in their downfalls to the end and are lost. With respect to themselves this not only easily could happen, but also undoubtedly would happen; but with respect to God it cannot possibly happen, since his plan cannot be changed, his promise cannot fail, the calling according to his purpose cannot be revoked, the merit of Christ as well as his interceding and preserving cannot be nullified, and the sealing of the Holy Spirit can neither be invalidated nor wiped out.

Article 9: *The Assurance of This Preservation*

Concerning this preservation of those chosen to salvation and concerning the perseverance of true believers in faith, believers themselves can and do become assured in accordance with the measure of their faith, by which they firmly believe that they are and always will remain true and living members of the church, and that they have the forgiveness of sins and eternal life.

Article 10: *The Ground of This Assurance*

Accordingly, this assurance does not derive from some private revelation beyond or outside the Word, but from faith in the promises of God which he has very plentifully revealed in his Word for our comfort, from the testimony of *the Holy Spirit testifying with our spirit that we are God's children and heirs* (Rom. 8:16–17), and finally from a serious and holy pursuit of a clear conscience and of good works. And if God's chosen ones in this world did not have this well-founded comfort that the victory will be theirs and this reliable guarantee of eternal glory, they would be of all people most miserable.

Article 11: *Doubts Concerning This Assurance*

Meanwhile, Scripture testifies that believers have to contend in this life with various doubts of the flesh and that under severe temptation they do not always experience this full assurance of faith and certainty of perseverance. But God, the Father of all comfort, *does not let them be tempted beyond what they can bear, but with the temptation he also provides a way out* (1 Cor. 10:13), and by the Holy Spirit revives in them the assurance of their perseverance.

Article 12: *This Assurance as an Incentive to Godliness*

This assurance of perseverance, however, so far from making true believers proud and carnally self-assured, is rather the true root of humility, of childlike respect, of genuine godliness, of endurance in every conflict, of fervent prayers, of steadfastness in crossbearing and in confessing the truth, and of well-founded joy in God. Reflecting on this benefit provides an incentive to a serious and continual practice of thanksgiving and good works, as is evident from the testimonies of Scripture and the examples of the saints.

Article 13: *Assurance No Inducement to Carelessness*

Neither does the renewed confidence of perseverance produce immorality or lack of concern for godliness in those put back on their feet after a fall, but it produces a much greater concern to observe carefully the ways of the Lord which he prepared in advance. They observe these ways in order that by walking in them they may maintain the assurance of their perseverance, lest, by their abuse of his fatherly goodness, the face of the gracious God (for the godly, looking upon his face is sweeter than life, but its withdrawal is more bitter than death) turn away from them again, with the result that they fall into greater anguish of spirit.

Article 14: *God's Use of Means in Perseverance*

And, just as it has pleased God to begin this work of grace in us by the proclamation of the gospel, so he preserves, continues, and completes his work by the hearing and reading of the gospel, by meditation on it, by its exhortations, threats, and promises, and also by the use of the sacraments.

Article 15: *Contrasting Reactions to the Teaching of Perseverance*

This teaching about the perseverance of true believers and saints, and about their assurance of it—a teaching which God has very richly revealed in his Word for the glory of his name and for the comfort of the godly and which he impresses on the hearts of believers—is something which the flesh does not understand, Satan hates, the world ridicules, the ignorant and the hypocrites abuse, and the spirits of error attack. The bride of Christ, on the other hand, has always loved this teaching very tenderly and defended it steadfastly as a priceless treasure; and God, against whom no plan can avail and no strength can prevail, will ensure that she will continue to do this. To this God alone, Father, Son, and Holy Spirit, be honor and glory forever. Amen.

*Rejection of the Errors
Concerning the Teaching of
the Perseverance of the Saints*

Having set forth the orthodox teaching, the Synod rejects the errors of those

I

Who teach that the perseverance of true believers is not an effect of election or a gift of God produced by Christ's death, but a condition of the new covenant which man, before what they call his "peremptory" election and justification, must fulfill by his free will.

For Holy Scripture testifies that perseverance follows from election and is granted to the chosen by virtue of Christ's death, resurrection, and intercession: *The chosen obtained it; the others were hardened* (Rom. 11:7); likewise, *He who did not spare his own son, but gave him up for us all—how will he not, along with him, grant us all things? Who will bring any charge against those whom God has chosen? It is God who justifies. Who is he that condemns? It is Christ Jesus who died—more than that, who was raised—who also sits at the right hand of God, and is also interceding for us. Who shall separate us from the love of Christ?* (Rom. 8:32–35).

II

Who teach that God does provide the believer with sufficient strength to persevere and is ready to preserve this strength in him if he performs his duty, but that even with all those things in place which are necessary to persevere in faith and which God is pleased to use to preserve faith, it still always depends on the choice of man's will whether or not he perseveres.

For this view is obviously Pelagian; and though it intends to make men free it makes them sacrilegious. It is against the enduring consensus of evangelical teaching which takes from man all cause for boasting and ascribes the praise for this benefit only to God's grace. It is also against the testimony of the apostle: *It is God who keeps us strong to the end, so that we will be blameless on the day of our Lord Jesus Christ* (1 Cor. 1:8).

III

Who teach that those who truly believe and have been born again not only can forfeit justifying faith as well as grace and salvation totally and to the end, but also in actual fact do often forfeit them and are lost forever.

For this opinion nullifies the very grace of justification and regeneration as well as the continual preservation by Christ, contrary to the plain words of the apostle Paul: *If Christ died for us while we were still sinners, we will therefore much more be saved from God's wrath through him, since we have now been justified by his blood* (Rom. 5:8–9); and contrary to the apostle John: *No one who is born of God is intent on sin, because God's seed remains in him, nor can he sin, because he has been born of God* (1 John 3:9); also contrary to the words of Jesus Christ: *I give eternal life to my sheep, and they shall never perish; no one can snatch them out of my hand. My Father, who has given them to me, is greater than all; no one can snatch them out of my Father's hand* (John 10:28–29).

IV

Who teach that those who truly believe and have been born again can commit the sin that leads to death (the sin against the Holy Spirit).

For the same apostle John, after making mention of those who commit the sin that leads to death and forbidding prayer for them (1 John 5:16–17), immediately adds: *We know that anyone born of God does not commit sin* (that is, that kind of sin), *but the one who was born of God keeps himself safe, and the evil one does not touch him* (v. 18).

V

Who teach that apart from a special revelation no one can have the assurance of future perseverance in this life.

For by this teaching the well-founded consolation of true believers in this life is taken away and the doubting of the Romanists is reintroduced into the church. Holy Scripture, however, in many places derives the assurance not from a special and extraordinary revelation but from the marks peculiar to God's children and from God's completely reliable promises. So especially the apostle Paul: *Nothing in all creation can separate us from the love of God that is in Christ Jesus our Lord* (Rom. 8:39); and John: *They who obey his commands remain in him and he in them. And this is how we know that he remains in us: by the Spirit he gave us* (1 John 3:24).

VI

Who teach that the teaching of the assurance of perseverance and of salvation is by its very nature and character an opiate of the flesh and is harmful to godliness, good morals, prayer, and other holy exercises, but that, on the contrary, to have doubt about this is praiseworthy.

For these people show that they do not know the effective operation of God's grace and the work of the indwelling Holy Spirit, and they contradict the apostle John, who asserts the opposite in plain words: *Dear friends, now we are children of God, but what we will be has not yet been made known. But we know that when he is made known, we shall be like him, for we shall see him as he is. Everyone who has this hope in him purifies himself, just as he is pure* (1 John 3:2–3). Moreover, they are refuted by the examples of the saints in both the Old and the New Testament, who though assured of their perseverance and salvation yet were constant in prayer and other exercises of godliness.

VII

Who teach that the faith of those who believe only temporarily does not differ from justifying and saving faith except in duration alone.

For Christ himself in Matthew 13:20 ff. and Luke 8:13 ff. clearly defines these further differences between temporary and true believers: he says that the former receive the seed on rocky ground, and the latter receive it in good ground, or a good heart; the former have no root, and the latter are firmly rooted; the former have no fruit, and the latter produce fruit in varying measure, with steadfastness, or perseverance.

VIII

Who teach that it is not absurd that a person, after losing his former regeneration, should once again, indeed quite often, be reborn.

For by this teaching they deny the imperishable nature of God's seed by which we are born again, contrary to the testimony of the apostle Peter: *Born again, not of perishable seed, but of imperishable* (1 Pet. 1:23).

IX

Who teach that Christ nowhere prayed for an unfailing perseverance of believers in faith.

For they contradict Christ himself when he says: *I have prayed for you, Peter, that your faith may not fail* (Luke 22:32); and John the gospel writer when he testifies in John 17 that it was not only for the apostles, but also for all those who were to believe by their message that Christ prayed: *Holy Father, preserve them in your name* (v. 11); and *My prayer is not that you take them out of the world, but that you preserve them from the evil one* (v. 15).

Conclusion

Rejection of False Accusations

And so this is the clear, simple, and straightforward explanation of the orthodox teaching on the five articles in dispute in the Netherlands, as well as the rejection of the errors by which the Dutch churches have for some time been disturbed. This explanation and rejection the Synod declares to be derived from God's Word and in agreement with the confessions of the Reformed churches. Hence it clearly appears that those of whom one could hardly expect it have shown no truth, equity, and charity at all in wishing to make the public believe:

—that the teaching of the Reformed churches on predestination and on the points associated with it by its very nature and tendency draws the minds of people away from all godliness and religion, is an opiate of the flesh and the devil, and is a stronghold of Satan where he lies in wait for all people, wounds most of them, and fatally pierces many of them with the arrows of both despair and self-assurance;
—that this teaching makes God the author of sin, unjust, a tyrant, and a hypocrite; and is nothing but a refurbished Stoicism, Manicheism, Libertinism, and Mohammedanism;
—that this teaching makes people carnally self-assured, since it persuades them that nothing endangers the salvation of the chosen, no matter how they live, so that they may commit the most outrageous crimes with self-assurance; and that on the other hand nothing is of use to the reprobate for salvation even if they have truly performed all the works of the saints;
—that this teaching means that God predestined and created, by the bare and unqualified choice of his will, without the least regard or consideration of any sin, the greatest part of the world to eternal condemnation; that in the same manner in which election is the source and cause of faith and good works, reprobation is the cause of unbelief and ungodliness; that many infant children of believers are snatched in their innocence from their mothers' breasts and cruelly cast into hell so that neither the blood of Christ nor their baptism nor the prayers of the church at their baptism can be of any use to them;

and very many other slanderous accusations of this kind which the Reformed churches not only disavow but even denounce with their whole heart.

Therefore this Synod of Dort in the name of the Lord pleads with all who devoutly call on the name of our Savior Jesus Christ to form their judgment about the faith of the Reformed churches, not on the basis of false accusations gathered from here or there, or even on the basis of the personal statements of a number of ancient and modern authorities— statements which are also often either quoted out of context or misquoted and twisted to convey a different meaning— but on the basis of the churches' own official confessions and of the present explanation of the orthodox teaching which has been endorsed by the unanimous consent of the members of the whole Synod, one and all.

Moreover, the Synod earnestly warns the false accusers themselves to consider how heavy a judgment of God awaits those who give false testimony against so many churches and their confessions, trouble the consciences of the weak, and seek to prejudice the minds of many against the fellowship of true believers.

Finally, this Synod urges all fellow ministers in the gospel of Christ to deal with this teaching in a godly and reverent manner, in the academic institutions as well as in the churches; to do so, both in their speaking and writing, with a view to the glory of God's name, holiness of life, and the comfort of anxious souls; to think and also speak with Scripture according to the analogy of faith; and, finally, to refrain from all those ways of speaking which go beyond the bounds set for us by the genuine sense of the Holy Scriptures and which could give impertinent sophists a just occasion to scoff at the teaching of the Reformed churches or even to bring false accusations against it.

May God's Son Jesus Christ, who sits at the right hand of God and gives gifts to men, sanctify us in the truth, lead to the truth those who err, silence the mouths of those who lay false accusations against sound teaching, and equip faithful ministers of his Word with a spirit of wisdom and discretion, that all they say may be to the glory of God and the building up of their hearers. Amen.

HARMONY OF HEIDELBERG CATECHISM
BELGIC CONFESSION AND THE CANONS OF DORT

This "Harmony of the Confessions," based on the order of the Heidelberg Catechism, is intended to serve as an aid in locating related statements of doctrine found in the other confessions. However, a word of caution is in order. Each of the confessions has its own peculiar function, since each was designed to meet specific needs of the church at a given time. A harmony of the confessions can be used with profit only when the independence and integrity of each confession is respected.

Heidelberg Catechism (Lord's Day) (Question & Answer)		Belgic Confession (Article)	Canons of Dort (Head & Article) (RE = Rejection of Errors)
I	1	—	I, 12–14; RE I, 6, 7; III/IV, 11; V, 8–12; RE V, 5
	2	—	I, 1–4. (Note: Each chapter follows order of sin, deliverance, gratitude.)
II	3	—	III/IV, 5, 6
	4	—	—
	5	14, 15	III/IV, 3–6; V, 2, 3
III	6	14	III/IV, 1
	7	14, 15	I, 1; III/IV, 1–4
	8	14, 15, 24	III/IV, 3, 4
IV	9	14, 15, 16	I, 1; III/IV, 1
	10	15, 37	I, 4; II, 1; III/IV, 1
	11	16, 17, 20	I, 1–4; II, 1, 2
V	12	20	II, 1
	13	14	II, 2; III/IV, 1–4
	14	—	—
	15	19	II, 1–4
VI	16	18, 19, 20, 21	II, 1–4
	17	19	II, 1–4
	18	10, 18, 19, 20, 21	II, 1–4
	19	2, 3, 4, 5, 6, 7	I, 3; II, 5; III/IV, 6–8
VII	20	22	I, 1–5; II, 5–7; III/IV, 6
	21	23, 24	III/IV, 9–14; RE III/IV, 6
	22	7	I, 3; II, 5; III/IV, 6–8
	23	9	—
VIII	24	8, 9	—
	25	8 9	—
IX	26	12, 13	—

Heidelberg Catechism (Lord's Day) (Question & Answer)		*Belgic Confession* (Article)	*Canons of Dort* (Head & Article) (RE = Rejection of Errors)
X	27	13	—
	28	12, 13	—
XI	29	21, 22	II, 3
	30	21, 22, 24	II, 5; RE II, 3–6
XII	31	21, 26	—
	32	—	V, 1, 2
XIII	33	10, 18, 19	—
	34	—	—
XIV	35	18, 19, 26	—
	36	18, 19	—
XV	37	20, 21	II, 2–4
	38	21	—
	39	20, 21	II, 2–4
XVI	40	20, 21	II, 3, 4; RE II, 7
	41	—	—
	42	—	—
	43	—	II, 8
	44	21	II, 4
XVII	45	20	RE, V, 1
XVIII	46	26	—
	47	19, 26	—
	48	19, 26	—
	49	26	—
XIX	50	26	—
	51	—	V, 1–15
	52	37	—
XX	53	11, 24	III/IV, 11, 12; RE III/IV, 5–8; V, 6, 7
XXI	54	16, 27, 28, 29	I, 1–18; II, 1–9; V, 9
	55	28, 30, 31	—
	56	22, 23	II, 7, 8; V, 5
XXII	57	37	—
	58	37	—
XXIII	59	21, 22, 23	II, 7, 8
	60	21, 22, 23	II, 7, 8
	61	21, 22, 23	II, 7, 8; RE II, 4
XXIV	62	23	II, 1; III/IV, 3–6; RE III/IV, 4, 5
	63	24	—
	64	24	III/IV, 11; V, 12, 13; RE V, 6

Heidelberg Catechism (Lord's Day) (Question & Answer)		Belgic Confession (Article)	Canons of Dort (Head & Article) (RE = Rejection of Errors)
XXV	65	24,33	III/IV, 17; RE III/IV, 7–9; V, 14
	66	33	—
	67	33	—
	68	33	—
XXVI	69	15, 34	—
	70	15, 34	—
	71	15, 34	—
XXVII	72	34	—
	73	34	—
	74	15, 34	I, 17
XXVIII	75	35	—
	76	35	—
	77	—	
XXIX	78	35	—
	79	35	—
XXX	80	35	—
	81	35	—
	82	35	—
XXXI	83	29, 30, 32	—
	84	29, 32	—
	85	29,32	—
XXXII	86	24	III/IV, 11, 12; V, 10, 12
	87	24	—
XXXIII	88	24	III/IV, 11, 12; V, 5, 7
	89	24	III/IV, 11, 12; V, 5, 7
	90	24	III/IV, 11, 12; V, 5, 7
	91	24, 25	—
XXXIV	92	—	—
	93	—	—
	94	1	—
	95	1	—
XXXV	96	32	—
	97	—	—
	98	7	III/IV, 17; V, 14
XXXVI	99	—	—
	100	—	—
XXXVII	101	36	—
	102	—	—
XXX-VIII	103	—	V, 14
XXXIX	104	36	—

Heidelberg Catechism (Lord's Day) (Question & Answer)		Belgic Confession (Article)	Canons of Dort (Head & Article) (RE = Rejection of Errors)
XL	105	36	—
	106	—	—
	107	—	—
XLI	108	—	—
	109	—	—
XLII	110	—	—
	111	—	—
XLIII	112	—	—
XLIV	113	—	—
	114	24, 29	V, 4
	115	25	III/IV, 17
XLV	116	—	—
	117	—	—
	118	—	—
	119	—	—
XLVI	120	12, 13, 36	—
	121	13	—
XLVII	122	2, 7	—
XLVIII	123	36, 37	—
XLIX	124	12, 24	III/IV, 11, 16
L	125	13	—
LI	126	15, 21, 22, 23	II, 7
LII	127	26	V, 6–8
	128	26	—
	129	—	—